DENISE SAMSON

LACE
KNITTING

40 OPENWORK PATTERNS, 30 LOVELY PROJECTS, COUNTLESS IDEAS AND INSPIRATION

Search Press

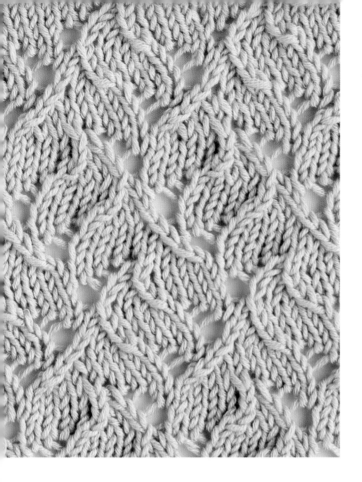

First published in Great Britain in 2019 by
Search Press Ltd
Wellwood, North Farm Road
Tunbridge Wells, Kent TN2 3DR

Originally published in Norwegian as *Hekta på hullstrikk*.

Also published in the United States of America in 2019 by
Trafalgar Square Books
North Pomfret, Vermont 05053

ISBN: 978-1-78221-813-5

Suppliers
For details of suppliers, please visit the Search Press website:
www.searchpress.com

Printed in China

CONTENTS

PREFACE

Lace knitting (known as *hullstrikk* or *blondestrikk* in Norwegian) has always fascinated me. When I was little, my mother knitted one shawl after the other, usually in very simple lace designs. She taught me the technique when I was school-age, and I remember when we advanced from shawls to bed jackets (a type of bolero, also called a soul warmer). They were knitted in one piece from sleeve to sleeve. The pattern consisted of four rows of garter stitch, a lace row with white yarn, and then a change to a new color, usually a pastel. (That pattern reminds me a little of the lace rows on the bed coverlet, The Sacred Tree, which you'll find on page 137.) Every single morning, my mother ate her breakfast in bed with the newspaper, wearing her bed jacket. She was never an expert knitter, but she gladdened many friends with shawls and soul warmers. This book would never have existed without her.

Writing a book is a time-consuming process, and it often happens that some of the yarns or colors used have gone out of production during the time between the making of the design and the printing of the book. With all the pretty yarns available in both yarn shops and on the internet, you shouldn't have trouble finding another yarn you like to use as a substitute. Check the ball band of the yarn you want to substitute, and make sure you achieve the correct gauge. (Read more about gauge on page 6.)

In the first part of this book, you'll find 40 different lace patterns—edgings, panels, and motif and cable patterns. Each pattern has a name. Some are well-known and have been knitted many times over the years, such as Sea Foam and Falling Leaves, while others are brand-new patterns of my own design. I've named these after whatever it is I thought they most resembled. In the second section, I'll show you how you can use these different patterns—either alone, or in combination, as for the Dress with Lupine Pattern on page 107 and the Lace Bonanza Tunic on page 145. If you've never knitted lace before, I recommend you begin by knitting some of the smaller, simpler pieces in the book before you throw yourself at the larger garments or bed coverings. First of all, though, you should learn what the chart symbols mean. That's explained for you on page 13.

I hope you'll find as much happiness in lace knitting as I have. One thing's for sure—you'll have earned yourself my heartfelt congratulations when you finish your first knitted piece with lace.

A LITTLE HISTORY

Lace knitting can be found in many places: in the Baltic countries and on the Shetland Islands, as well as in southern Europe. In the spring of 2017, I spent an entire week in Shetland participating in the Summer Academy (sommerakademiet.com), and learned a lot about lace knitting. I was able to see the most fantastic work, knitted with incredibly finely-spun gossamer yarn on very thin needles.

No one knows how lace knitting came to Shetland, but the oldest piece we know of, a christening hat with what's known as a "spider" pattern, is believed to have been knitted in the 1830s. At that time, women on Shetland had little or no money for food, clothing, or items for the house and home, but they could knit! With the most beautiful patterns, worked with astoundingly delicate needles and yarn, they magically produced one garment after another, each finer than the last. The more delicately and more thinly they knitted, the higher the price for which the resulting work could be sold. We should also note cultural variations; in Italy and Spain, where lace knitting originated, lace was produced for the church, knitted by nuns and women from the aristocracy who had plenty of time. The patterns often had long repeats, with more than 50 stitches and 100 or more rows. These women were well-educated and could both read and write their own patterns.

Women living in Shetland were much poorer and often illiterate, and used their ingenuity to design simple patterns that could be combined for carefully composed pieces. The patterns were seldom more than 10-12 different stitch or pattern rows, but the arrangement of the various repeats

meant their work looked much more complicated than it was. They often knitted reversible pieces with lace on both the right and wrong sides. Work knitted with lace only on the right side of the piece was called "lazy lace." The most impressive item I saw in the museums I visited was a bridal shawl knitted on very fine needles with yarn as thin as sewing thread. The shawl measures 2.2 x 2.2 yd / 2 x 2 meters, and is so fine you could pull it through a wedding ring! There were very few who could spin the yarn used to make such a thing, and very few knitters capable of knitting such a masterpiece. The yarn was spun from the finest fibers available, namely the neck wool of sheep. It must have taken a long time to produce such a shawl. Yarn would have been spun over the winter in preparation, and the shawl itself would have been knitted during the summer, when daylight lasted for about 20 hours. A total of at least a year would have been necessary to produce a shawl like this, from preparing and spinning the wool to the finished knitting.

You can still buy lovely shawls and other lace work in Shetland, and with today's technology, the shawls can be knitted on modern knitting machines, which are able to precisely reproduce the patterns of hand-knitted pieces. I met many lovely women during my stay on Shetland; some knitted by machine, but the oldest women still knitted these beautiful patterns by hand.

Now it's your turn to knit some of the charming patterns I've collected in this book.

Good luck!

Denise Samson

> Denise Samson on the internet:
> www.andreboller.no
> Facebook: Denise Samson Design
> Instagram: @denisesamson56

KNITTING GAUGE

If you want good results from your knitting, you must obtain the correct gauge = UK tension. Before you begin knitting a new project, knit a gauge swatch. A good rule of thumb is to read through the whole pattern before you start knitting. There are often several steps that must be worked at the same time, and it's irritating to discover too late that you've skipped over some instructions or made a mistake—no one ever wants to have to rip out hard work. The band around a ball of yarn (the ball band) always lists the recommended needle size and number of stitches in 4 in / 10 cm. In most patterns (and all the patterns in this book) you'll be given the gauge the designer worked with. For example, 22 stitches on needles that are U. S. size 4 / 3.5 mm = 4 in / 10 cm. Sometimes you'll also be given a row/round gauge, which tells you how many rows/rounds should fit into 4 in / 10 cm in length; but this is less relevant, since most patterns list length in inches or centimeters rather than numbers of rows or rounds. However, if the row/round gauge is listed in a pattern, it's important!

Cast on a few more stitches than recommended for 4 in / 10 cm and work the swatch until it's square. If there's a row/round gauge included, knit 2 in / 5 cm more than given for 4 in / 10 cm. Use a measuring tape or ruler and measure 4 in / 10 cm in width. Place a pin at each end. That way it'll be easy to count the number of stitches in 4 in / 10 cm. If your count adds up to too many stitches, it means you've knitted too tightly and should go up a needle size. If there are too few stitches in 4 in / 10 cm, then you've knitted too loosely and should try smaller needles. It's especially important to maintain the gauge if you want to knit in a particular size. This isn't as important when you are knitting a blanket or a scarf, a hand towel or washcloth; but it's worth the trouble for fitted garments of any kind. You may think it's tedious to knit a gauge swatch—but I can promise you it's even more annoying to knit a large project like a dress or a sweater and then discover it doesn't fit!

If you want to change the look of a design, though, it can be fun to experiment with needle sizes other than those recommended for the yarn. Here you can see examples of how a pattern can change when you knit with different needle sizes. The yarn I used here was Lille Lerke from Dale, which has a recommended needle size of U. S. 1.5-2.5 / 2.5-3 mm.

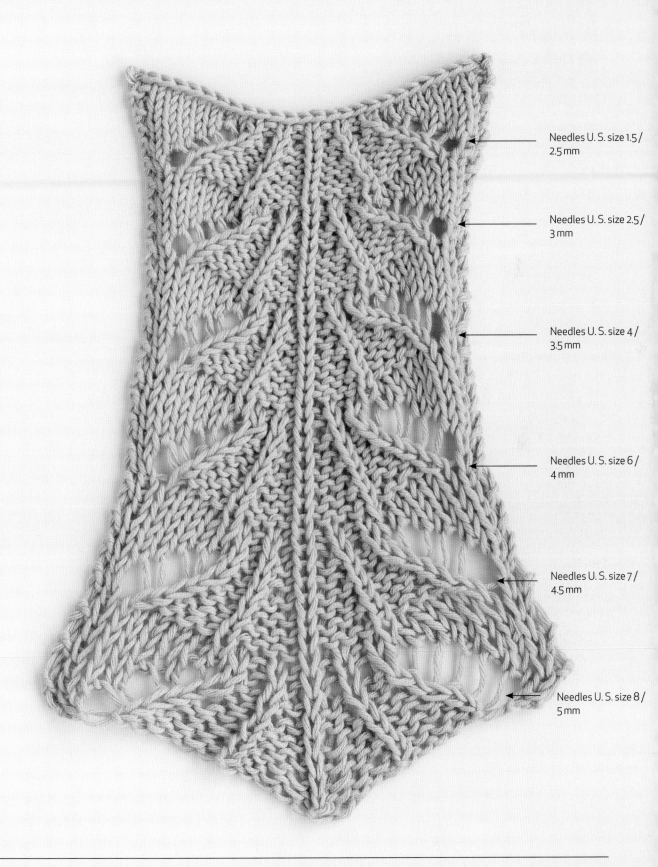

Needles U. S. size 1.5 / 2.5 mm

Needles U. S. size 2.5 / 3 mm

Needles U. S. size 4 / 3.5 mm

Needles U. S. size 6 / 4 mm

Needles U. S. size 7 / 4.5 mm

Needles U. S. size 8 / 5 mm

VARYING PATTERN APPEARANCE

Sometimes it can be fun to experiment with a pattern in a variety of yarn sizes and qualities. As an example, I knitted the same pattern with four different yarn types and needle sizes.

See also the Rugged Sweater with Medallion Patterns on page 157 and the Yoked Dress on page 107, both of which are knitted with the Medallion pattern (no. 31). Despite the shared design element, they look very different, because the dress is knitted with needles U. S. size 2.5 / 3 mm while the sweater is worked with heavy yarn on large needles (Anouk on U. S. 15 / 10 mm).

This sample is knitted with Gamma from Lang Yarns on needles U. S. size 8 / 5 mm

Swatch knitted with Kid Seta from Mondial on needles U. S. size 6 / 4 mm

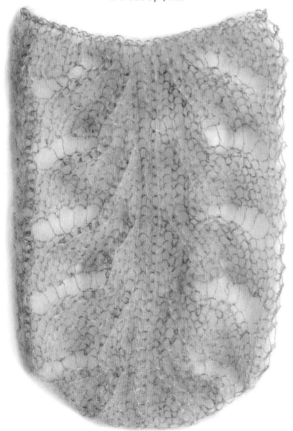

Sample knitted with Lille Lerke from Dale Yarn on needles U. S. size 2.5 / 3 mm

Swatch knitted with Anouk from Lang Yarns on needles U. S. size 13 / 9 mm

HOW TO READ CHARTS

When reading a book or other text in English, you usually begin at the top left and read to the right and down. Charts are read in the opposite way: you begin at the bottom right and progress towards the left. When knitting back and forth, you read the second line from left to right. If you're working in the round, you always read from right to left. Every square on the chart has a symbol with an explanation (see next page). This can look very confusing if you aren't familiar with knitting charts, but you can learn to read them just as easily as paragraphs with some practice. Here you see an example of how a chart with symbols and explanations can look. The area outlined with red shows a complete repeat on the chart. On this chart, four repeats are shown, one after the other.

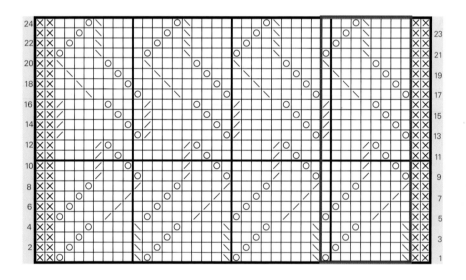

☐ Knit on RS, purl on WS

☒ Purl on RS, knit on WS

◺ RS: Sl 1, k1, psso; WS: p2tog tbl

◹ RS: k2tog; WS: p2tog

⊙ Yarnover

If this chart were written out, it would look like this:

Row 1: P2 (sl 1, k1, psso, k7, yo) 4 times, p2.
Row 2: K2, (p1, yo, p6, p2tog tbl) 4 times, k2.
Row 3: P2, (sl 1, k1, psso, k5, yo, k2) 4 times, p2.
Row 4: K2, (p3, yo, 4, p2tog tbl) 4 times, k2.
Row 5: P2, (k3, k2tog, k4, yo) 4 times, p2.
Row 6: K2, (p1, yo, p4, p2tog, p2) 4 times, k2.
Row 7: P2, (k1, k2tog, k4, yo, k2) 4 times, p2.
Row 8: K2, (p3, yo, p4, k2tog) 4 times, k2.

Row 9: P2, (yo, k3, k2tog, k4) 4 times, p2.
Row 10: K2, (p4, p2tog, p2, yo, p1) 4 times, k2.
Row 11: P2, (k2, yo, k1, k2tog, k4) 4 times, p2.
Row 12: K2, (p4, p2tog, yo, p3) 4 times, k2.
Row 13: P2, (yo, k7, k2tog) 4 times, p2.
Row 14: K2, (p2tog, p6, yo, p1) 4 times, k2.
Row 15: P2, (k2, yo, k5, k2tog) 4 times, p2.
Row 16: K2, (p2tog, p4, yo, p3), 4 times, k2.
Row 17: P2, (yo, k4, sl 1, k1, psso, k3) 4 times, p2.
Row 18: K2, (p2, p2tog tbl, p4, yo, p1) 4 times, k2.

Row 19: P2, (k2, yo, k4, sl 1, k1, psso, k1) 4 times, p2.
Row 20: K2, (p2tog tbl, p4, yo, p3) 4 times, k2.
Row 21: P2, (k4, sl 1, k1, psso, k3, yo) 4 times, p2.
Row 22: K2, (p1, yo, p2, p2tog tbl, p4) 4 times, k2.
Row 23: P2, (k4, sl 1, k1, psso, k1, yo, k2) 4 times, p2.
Row 24: K2, (p3, yo, p2tog tbl, p4) 4 times, k2.

As you can see, there's a lot more text to pay attention to; charts are a simple way to convey the same information as all this text at a glance.

When you set aside your work to do something else, it's a good idea to note down your place in the pattern or use a row counter (see page 14) to indicate which row or round you are on in the pattern. It isn't always easy to work out where you left off and what to do next when you're working lace. It might also be a good idea to take a photo of the chart you're working on with your smart phone or tablet, and then print out the photo; you can write on the printout or mark it up however you like, and take a new photo of the unmarked original if you need to.

ABBREVIATIONS

BO	bind off (= UK cast off)	**p2tog**	purl 2 sts together = 1 st decreased
CDD	centered double decrease: slip 2 sts knitwise at the same time, k1, psso.	**pm**	place marker
		psso	pass slipped st over
ch	chain st	**rem**	remain(s)(ing)
cm	centimeter(s)	**rep**	repeat(s)
CO	cast on	**rnd(s)**	round(s)
dc	double crochet (= UK treble crochet)	**RS**	right side
		sc	single crochet (= UK double crochet)
g	gram(s)	**sl**	slip
in	inch(es)	**sl m**	slip marker
k	knit	**ssk**	slip, slip, knit = (sl 1 knitwise) 2 times, knit the 2 sts together through back loops
k2tog	knit 2 sts together = 1 st decreased; right-leaning decrease		
kf&b	knit into front and then back of same stitch	**tbl**	through back loop(s)
		tog	together
		WS	wrong side
m	meter(s)	**yd**	yard(s)
mm	millimeter(s)	**yo**	yarnover

SYMBOLS KEY

There aren't many symbols to remember for lace knitting. I recommend that before you start a new pattern, you take the time to learn what the symbols mean on the chart you'll be working from. Below you'll see a list of the symbols used in this book. Each chart throughout the book also has a key for the symbols used on that chart, so you don't have to constantly refer back to this page.

▨	No stitch
☐	Knit on RS, purl on WS
Ⅱ	Knit on RS, knit on WS
⊠	Purl on RS, knit on WS
⊙	Yarnover
◺	Sl 1, k1, psso or k2tog tbl
◣	Ssk
⊿	K2tog on RS, p2tog on WS
◥	P2tog tbl
⬈	P2tog
⅄	K3tog
⅁	Sl 1, k2tog, psso
⋏	CDD
⧅	K1tob on RS, p1tbl on WS
▼	Kf&b
●	K5 into same st, alternating knitting into front and then back loop; turn and p5, turn ald k5tog.
⟍⟍	Place 1 knit and 2 purl sts on a cable needle and hold in front of work, k1, place the 2 purl sts back on left needle and p2, k1 from cable needle.
▭	Repeat

TOOLS

Needles

I'm rather picky when it comes to knitting needles, and I've invested in both aluminum and carbon needles. They're expensive, but I knit so much that having the correct and best tools is worth it for me to achieve good results. You undoubtedly have your own favorite needles that you like to use; the one thing I recommend is that you use distinctly pointed needles when knitting lace. It's easier to insert pointed needles into stitches when joining 2, 3, and 4 sts together. Avoid blunt-tipped needles. I also don't use straight needles when I knit, except for double-points. I always use circulars, even when knitting back and forth, because they cause less stress on my shoulders.

Blocking Mats
I have some blocking mats that join together like a jigsaw puzzle. The package came with a tape measure, long thin blocking wires, and special T-pins for blocking.

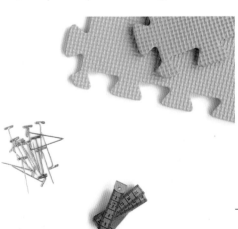

Stitch Markers

Stitch markers are a great help when knitting lace, especially when you're repeating a pattern with many stitches. If you make a mistake, you just have to count the stitches between the markers to see whether the error occurred in that repeat.

Row Counters

A row counter is also a great tool to have on hand. It can be hard to find your place in a lace pattern if you've set the work aside for a while. Set the row counter to the number on the right or left of the chart and you'll always know where to begin again. Some row counters can be placed on knitting needles.

Before blocking

BLOCKING

To achieve the best results with lace knitting, you'll need to block your work, particularly shawls, scarves, blankets, hand towels, and other rectangular pieces. Stitches often draw together in lace knitting, and it's easy to tell the difference between projects that have been blocked and projects that haven't.

If you want a professional result, follow these easy steps. You don't need specialized tools for blocking. You can just lay your work on a foam board or rubber mat, on a padded ironing board, or the mattress of your bed. You really only need pins for blocking (T-pins are my recommendation).

There are several ways to block lace knitting. Start by dampening the piece. If you prefer, you can soak the piece in lukewarm water with mild soap (Unicorn Fibre Wash, Soak, or Eucalan, for example) and then carefully squeeze out as much water as possible. You can also lay a damp towel over the work, or use a spray bottle with water to dampen the piece, and then lay it out for blocking. The most important factor is spreading the work out into the correct shape with blocking wires, or with pins on the blocking surface. Stretch the piece into shape and then secure it. Personally, I like to stretch out flat pieces—such as shawls, scarves, blankets, edgings, and panels—with pins, dampen them well with water from a spray bottle, and then let the item air dry. Once the piece is completely dry, I remove the pins. If I've knitted a sweater, dress, or something else on circular needles, however, I pat the piece out to its finished measurements and then lay a damp towel over it. Sometimes, I carefully steam press the work with a damp towel or pressing cloth over the piece. Some designs have points or wavy edges. Make sure you pin out those pieces well so the points or waves in the lace pattern will stay distinct after blocking.

Dampened and stretched with pins

Finished blocking

CORRECTING MISTAKES

It's essentially impossible to avoid making some mistakes when knitting lace. However, instead of ripping out the work every time, it may be possible to repair these mistakes. It's not the easiest thing to do with lace, though—deciding when it's worth ripping out instead of trying to fix an incorrectly-worked stitch depends on how far down in the work the mistake is.

The first indication something may be amiss is too few or too many stitches on the needle. If you have too many stitches, you've likely added one too many yarnovers. If there are too few stitches, perhaps you knitted three together instead of two, missed a stitch, or forgot a yarnover. The first thing you need to do is find the mistake. If you placed stitch markers between each repeat, it'll be relatively easy to find the section with the mistake. If not, you'll have to count stitches from the beginning of the row or round until you locate the error.

A Dropped Stitch
First and foremost, make sure the missing stitch hasn't dropped and run down. I use a crochet hook to catch the "lost" loop and then chain it back up into place. If several stitches have dropped down, I prefer to rip back to the row where the mistake is.

One Stitch Too Many
This is easy! Just skip the next yarnover. If you've already knitted a row or round or two past it, you can still skip a yarnover. Once you've blocked the piece or steam-pressed it, it won't be seen at all.

One Stitch Too Few
If you forgot a yarnover, you can fix that on the next pattern row or round. Just pick up the strand between the two stitches where there should have been a yarnover. If you forgot a yarnover two rows or rounds down, pick up the stitch with a crochet hook as for a dropped stitch and chain up.

One Too Many K2tog Stitches
You have two options here if the problem just happened. One option is to rip back; I unpick stitch by stitch rather than ripping out, because it's too complicated to catch all the stitches with yarnovers and k2tog. A second option is to make an extra stitch by picking up the strand between two stitches and knitting it through the back loop.

Parts of the Pattern Are Incorrect
If I spot an error far down in the piece—for example, the pattern has shifted somehow and no longer looks like the design I'm working—I rip out. First, though, I add a lifeline. Take a fine, smooth contrast color yarn longer than the width of the piece, and use a blunt tapestry needle to weave it through the right leg of each stitch on the row/round where the error appears. Be careful not to sew the lifeline through any stitches (splitting the yarn). Then go back to where you're working and start ripping out. The lifeline will prevent you from ripping out too far down, and at the same time you have the stitches secured so you can pick them up with the needle without losing any. Run the knitting needle along the lifeline, through the right leg of each stitch, until all the stitches have been retrieved, and then you'll be ready to start working again.

LACE PATTERNS
PART 1

For the most part, lace knitting consists of making yarnovers and corresponding k2tog decreases, so the stitch count remains consistent throughout even as the pattern made by the stitches shifts and changes. Sometimes, however, we need more yarnovers to shape the piece—for example, on edges with waves or points—and other times, we need to knit three stitches together and put a yarnover on each side.

In this section, I've collected 40 different lace designs, explained with symbols, short descriptions, and charts. Some of the patterns occur in ribbing, others in edgings, but most can cover an entire surface. You'll find these patterns used in Part 2, and you'll be able to see how varied these lace patterns look, whether they're knitted over a large surface or only a decorative detail in a piece.

My hope is that you'll be inspired to make your own designs, and that you can create lovely new pieces with the help of the different patterns you'll find in this book, composed from several charts or simply rearranged to suit your taste.

Edgings and Panels

The lace motifs on the following pages can be used for ribbed edgings or the edgings for blankets, ponchos, hand towels, etc.

NO. 1 FLOWER BUDS

I cast on 37 stitches for this sample. The chart shows 5 repeats across and 4 repeats in length. One repeat consists of 7 stitches and 4 rows. On page 15, you can see how this design looks before and after blocking.

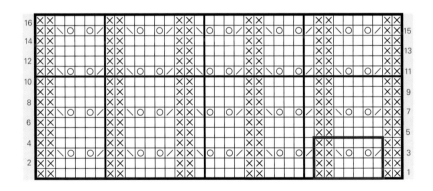

	Knit on RS, purl on WS
☒	Purl on RS, knit on WS
↘	Sl 1, k1, psso
↗	K2tog
⊙	Yo

NO. 2 LACE RIBBING

I cast on 36 stitches for this sample. The chart shows 4 repeats with 4 stitches in stockinette / stocking stitch between each lace repeat. The repeat has 4 stitches and 4 rows. This pattern was used for the Washcloth and Hand Towel set on page 97.

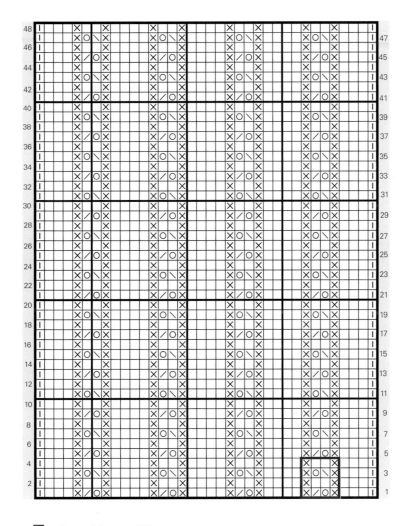

☐	Knit on RS, knit on WS
☐	Knit on RS, purl on WS
☒	Purl on RS, knit on WS
◺	Sl 1, k1, psso
◹	K2tog
◉	Yo

NO. 3 LACE STRIPES

I cast on 40 stitches for this sample. The chart shows 6 repeats in both width and length. One repeat consists of 6 stitches and 2 rows. You'll find this motif on the Christening Gown and Hat (see page 153).

- ☐ (I)   Knit on RS, knit on WS
- ☐   Knit on RS, purl on WS
- ☒   Purl on RS, knit on WS
- ◺   Sl 1, k1, psso
- ◹   K2tog
- ⊡   Yo

NO. 4 WATERFALL

For this sample, I cast on 39 stitches. On the chart, there are 45 stitches across, which is because the yarnovers on the 1st, 7th, and 13th rows add 6 stitches. The chart shows 6 repeats across, with 3 stitches in reverse stockinette / stocking stitch between each repeat, and 3 repeats in length. Repeats switch between 3 and 4 stitches across, and they are all 6 stitches in length. As you can see, there is a "blind" stitch on the 4th, 5th, and 6th rows of the pattern. The Lace Bonanza Tunic on page 145 utilizes this motif for the raglan shaping.

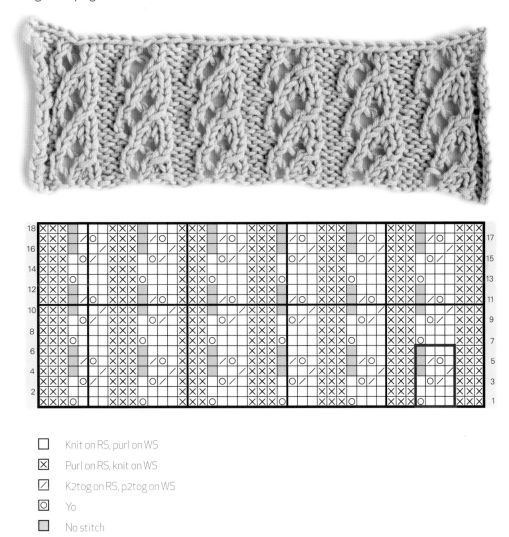

☐   Knit on RS, purl on WS

☒   Purl on RS, knit on WS

◢   K2tog on RS, p2tog on WS

⊡   Yo

▨   No stitch

NO. 5 CLIMBING ROSES

This swatch begins with 38 stitches cast on. The pattern is repeated 4 times on the chart, with 2 stitches in reverse stockinette / stocking stitch between each repeat. One repeat consists of 7 stitches and 8 rows. You'll find it used on the Long Lace Scarf (see page 161).

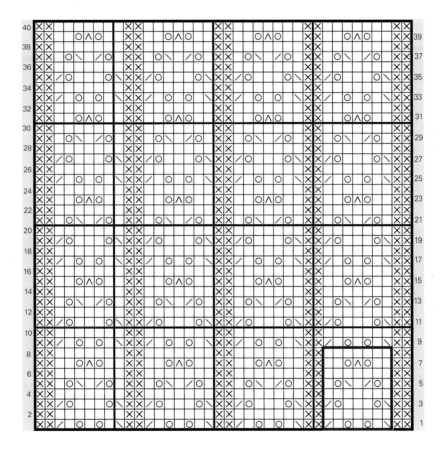

☐   Knit on RS, purl on WS

☒   Purl on RS, knit on WS

⊡   Yo

◺   Sl 1, k1, psso

◹   K2tog

◮   CDD

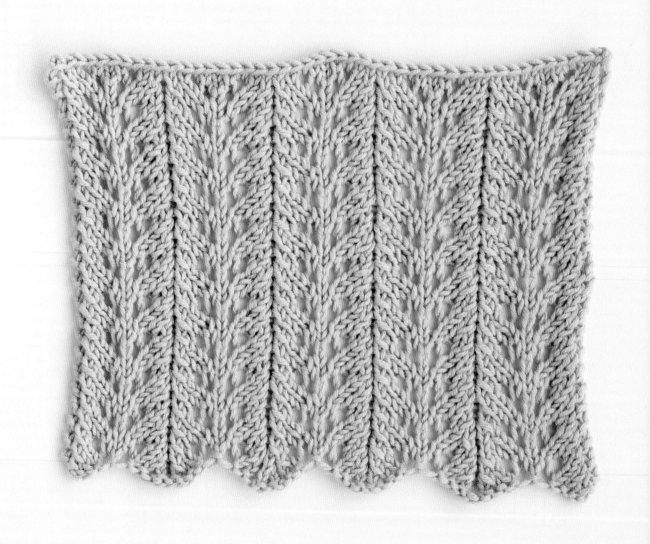

NO. 6 LUPINES

I cast on 47 stitches for this sample. The chart shows 5 repeats in width and 10 repeats in length. One repeat has 9 stitches and 4 rows. This pattern appears on the Girl's Sweater with Lupine Patterns on page 111.

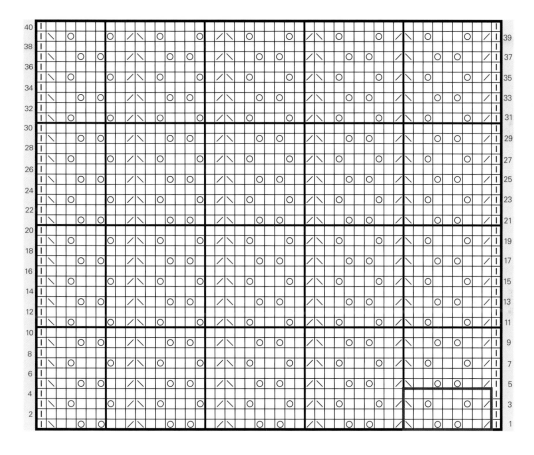

	Ⅰ	Knit on RS, knit on WS
	☐	Knit on RS, purl on WS
	◤	Sl 1, k1, psso
	◢	K2tog
	⊙	Yo

NO. 7 VIKING SHIP

I cast on 49 stitches for this swatch. The chart shows 3 repeats across and 1 repeat in length. One repeat has 15 stitches and 14 rows, with 1 stitch in stockinette / stocking stitch between each repeat. This pattern embellishes the lower edge of the Yoked Dress on page 107.

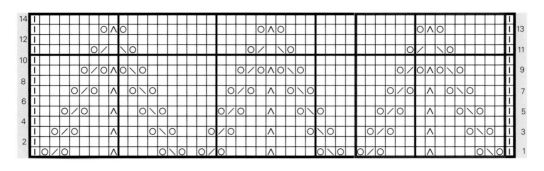

- ☐ Knit on RS, knit on WS
- ☐ Knit on RS, purl on WS
- ⊙ Yo
- ◺ Sl 1, k1, psso
- ◹ K2tog
- ◮ CDD

NO. 8 ROPE AND LACE

I cast on 13 stitches. The chart shows 1 repeat in width and 6 repeats in length. As you can see, you work lace on both the right and wrong sides. One repeat has 13 stitches and 6 rows. The Bookmark on page 133 is made with the Rope and Lace pattern.

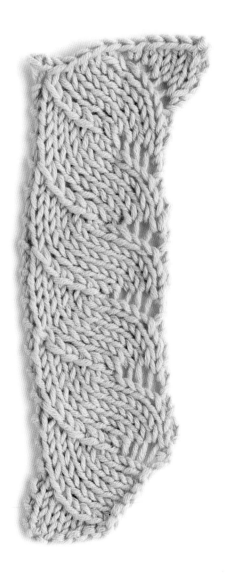

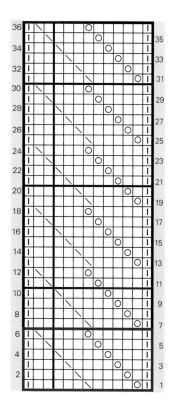

	Knit on RS, knit on WS
	Knit on RS, purl on WS
	On RS: Sl 1, k1, psso; on WS: p2tog tbl
	Yo

NO. 9 ZIGZAG EDGE

I began by casting on 13 stitches, but due to the increases and decreases on the chart, the stitch count changes from 13 to 20 stitches over a repeat. The chart shows 1 repeat across and 2 repeats in length. One repeat has between 13 and 20 stitches across and 30 rows in length. This pattern edges the Sacred Tree Coverlet on page 137.

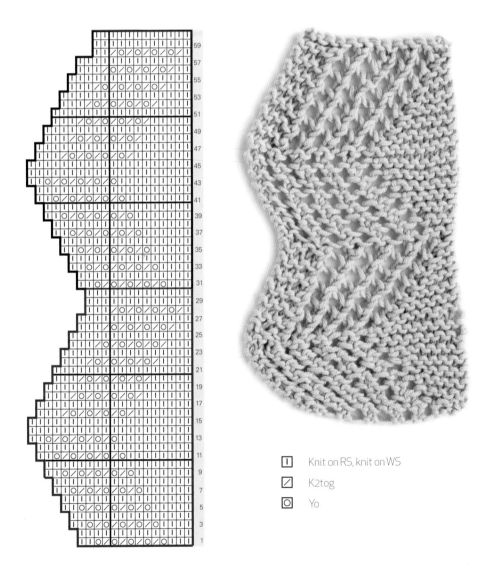

		Knit on RS, knit on WS
		K2tog
		Yo

NO. 10 WAVES AT THE BEACH

I cast on 12 stitches for this sample, but the stitch count changes from 12 to 17 stitches over a repeat because of increases and decreases (see chart). The chart shows 1 repeat across and 3 repeats in length. One repeat also has between 12 and 17 stitches across and 20 rows in length. The first two rows on the chart are worked only once. This pattern edges the Zigzag Shawl on page 115.

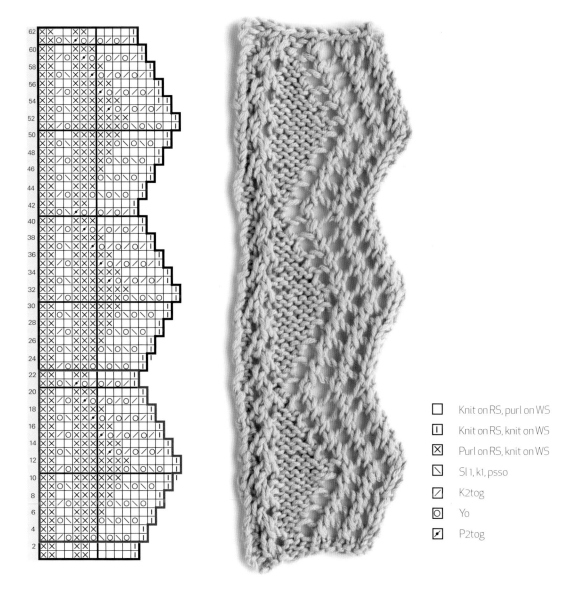

☐ Knit on RS, purl on WS

Ⅰ Knit on RS, knit on WS

☒ Purl on RS, knit on WS

◺ Sl 1, k1, psso

◿ K2tog

◉ Yo

◹ P2tog

NO. 11 EDGE WITH FAUX CABLE

I began by casting on 16 stitches, but due to increases and decreases (see chart), the stitch count changes from 13 to 18 stitches over the repeat. The chart shows 1 repeat across and 4 repeats in length. Each repeat consists of between 13 and 18 stitches across and 14 rows in length. The Poncho on page 163 is edged with this mock cable design.

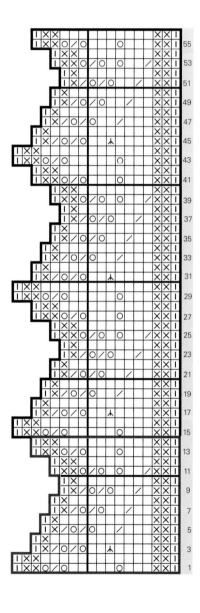

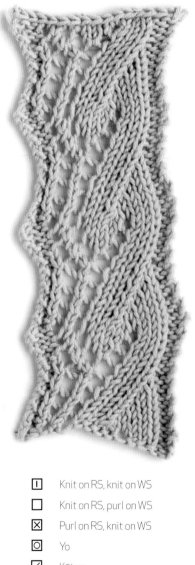

	▯	Knit on RS, knit on WS
	▢	Knit on RS, purl on WS
	☒	Purl on RS, knit on WS
	▢ (O)	Yo
	◪ (/)	K2tog
	⯅	K3tog

NO. 12 LACE EDGING

I cast on 18 stitches for this sample. The chart shows 1 repeat in width and 8 repeats in length. As for the previous pattern, the lace is worked on both right and wrong sides. One repeat has 18 stitches across and 6 rows. This pattern is used to edge the Skirt on page 129.

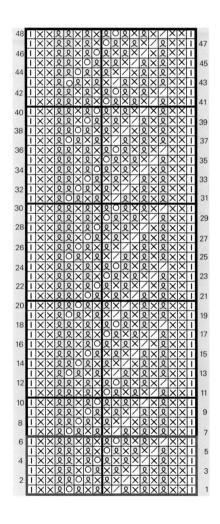

	Knit on RS, knit on WS
℧	Twisted knit (k1tbl) on RS, twisted purl (p1tbl) on WS
✕	Purl on RS, knit on WS
╱	K2tog on RS, p2tog on WS
○	Yo

Leaf Patterns

Leaf patterns are fun to knit. Some leaf designs show especially well when surrounded with reverse stockinette / stocking stitch, which raises the leaves on the surface.

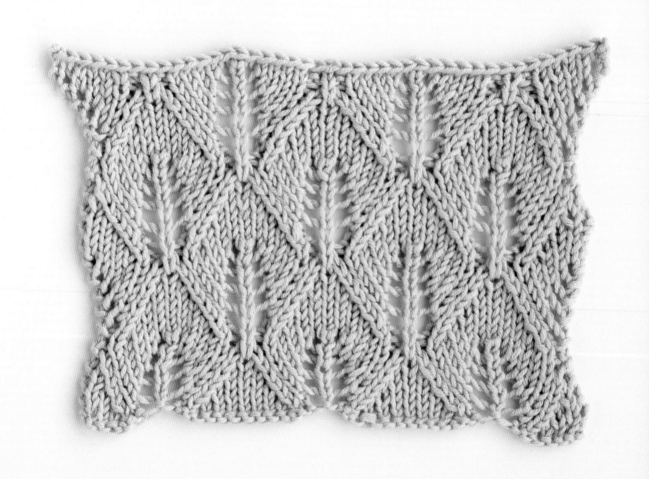

NO. 13 FALLING LEAVES

I cast on 43 stitches for this sample. The chart shows 3 repeats across and 2 in length. One repeat consists of 14 stitches and 20 rows. I used this pattern on the Lace Bonanza Tunic on page 145.

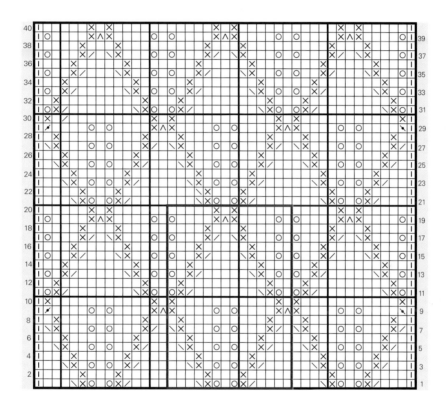

☐	Knit on RS, knit on WS
☐	Knit on RS, purl on WS
☒	Purl on RS, knit on WS
⟍	Sl 1, k1, psso
⟋	K2tog
⊙	Yo
⋀	CDD
⟋	P2tog tbl
⟍	P2tog

NO. 14 LEAF VINE

I cast on 37 sts for this swatch. The chart shows 3 repeats in length and 1 repeat across, with reverse stockinette / stocking stitch on each side to emphasize the leaf motif. One repeat is 13 sts and 16 rows. See how the pattern looks on the sleeves of the Sweater with Leafy Vines on page 103.

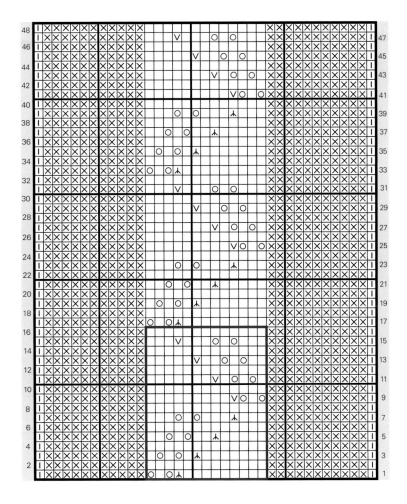

I	Knit on RS, knit on WS
☐	Knit on RS, purl on WS
☒	Purl on RS, knit on WS
☉	Yo
☑	Sl 1, k2tog, psso
⋏	K3tog

NO. 15 BIRCH LEAVES

This swatch begins with 35 stitches cast on. The chart shows 1 repeat across and 2 repeats in length. One repeat consists of 31 stitches and 18 rows. The pattern was used for the body of the Sweater with Leafy Vines on page 103.

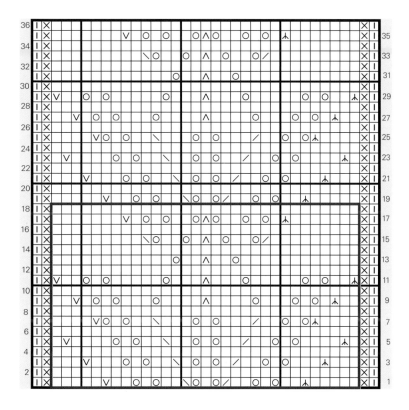

☐	Knit on RS, knit on WS
☐	Knit on RS, purl on WS
☒	Purl on RS, knit on WS
⟍	Sl 1, k1, psso
⟋	K2tog
◯	Yo
⋁	Sl 1, k2tog, psso
⋏	K3tog
⋀	CDD

NO. 16 THE SACRED TREE

I cast on 3 stitches and then gradually increased to 63 stitches before decreasing back to 3 stitches. Because this pattern is so large, I divided the patterning over Charts 1 and 2. **NOTE:** The decreases/reductions in stitch count occur on the wrong side on Chart 2. One stitch repeat varies from 3-63 stitches; there are 120 rows per repeat. This pattern is used for the Sacred Tree Coverlet (see page 137). The charts are on the next two pasges.

Chart 1

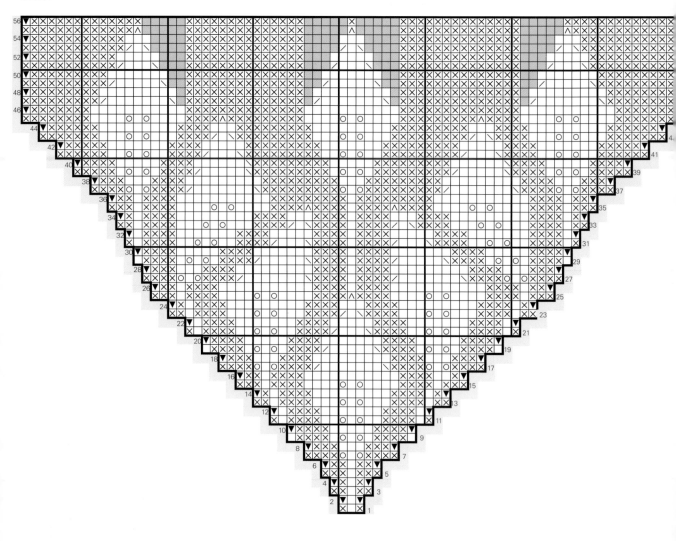

☐ Knit on RS, purl on WS

☒ Purl on RS, knit on WS

◺ Sl 1, k1, psso

◹ K2tog

⊙ Yo

◭ CDD

▼ Kf&b

▨ No stitch

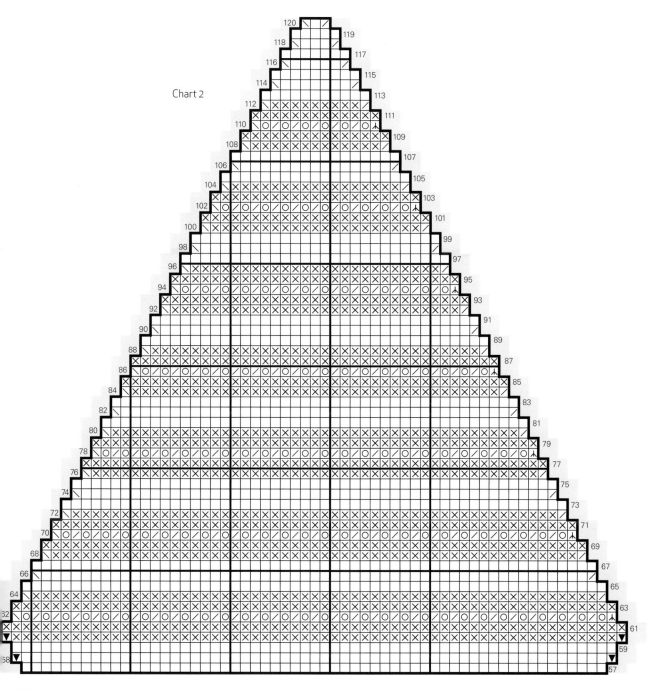

Chart 2

	Knit on RS, purl on WS
$\boxtimes$	Purl on RS, knit on WS
$\blacktriangledown$	Kf&b
$\diagdown$	Sl 1, k1, psso (worked on WS)
$\diagup$	K2tog (on WS)
$\boxed{\circ}$	Yo (on WS)
$\perp$	K3tog (on WS)

Diagonal Lace

Sometimes it isn't easy to see what a lace design will look like just from the chart, but you'll be able to pick out the hearts and flowers that appear on the charts in this section easily.

NO. 17 ZIGZAG

I cast on 30 stitches here. The chart shows 14 repeats across and 4 repeats in length. One repeat consists of 2 stitches and 12 rows. The lovely waves along each side are shown to advantage in the Zigzag Pattern Shawl on page 115.

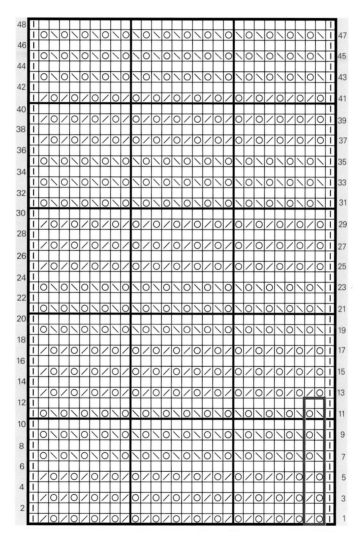

⊞	Knit on RS, knit on WS
□	Knit on RS, purl on WS
◺	Sl 1, k1, psso
◹	K2tog
⊙	Yo

NO. 18 CHICKEN TRACKS

I cast on 38 stitches for this sample. The chart shows 4 repeats across and 3 in length. One repeat has 9 stitches and 16 rows. See page 145 to take a look at how this pattern's used on the Lace Bonanza Tunic.

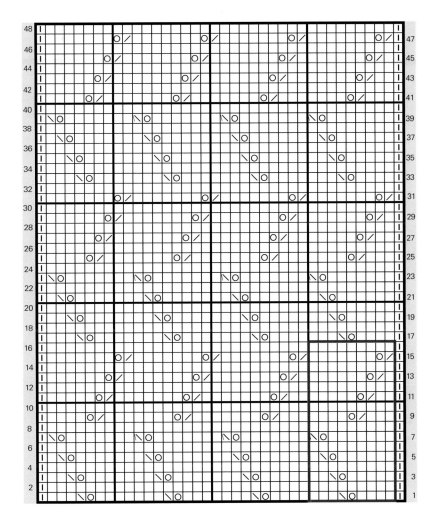

	Knit on RS, knit on WS
	Knit on RS, purl on WS
⊠	Purl on RS, knit on WS
⟍	Sl 1, k1, psso
⟋	K2tog
⊙	Yo

NO. 19 HARLEQUIN LACE

I cast on 37 stitches here. The chart shows 3 repeats in length and 1 repeat across, with reverse stockinette / stocking stitch on each side of the lace motif. One repeat is 19 stitches and 12 rows. This pattern appears on the Socks shown on page 123.

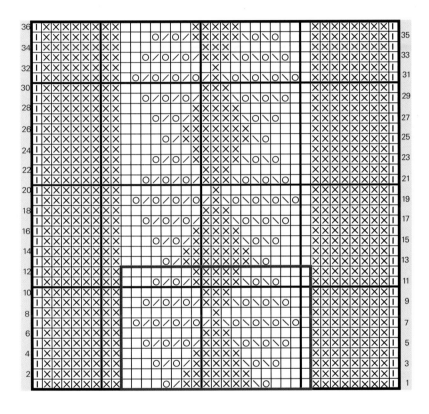

I	Knit on RS, knit on WS
☐	Knit on RS, purl on WS
☒	Purl on RS, knit on WS
◨	Sl 1, k1, psso
◨	K2tog
◉	Yo

NO. 20 SPRUCE

I cast on 27 stitches for this swatch. The chart shows 1 repeat across and 5 repeats in length. The repeat has 8 rows, but alternates between 25 and 27 stitches across. On page 8, you can see how this pattern differs when worked with a variety of yarns and needle sizes.

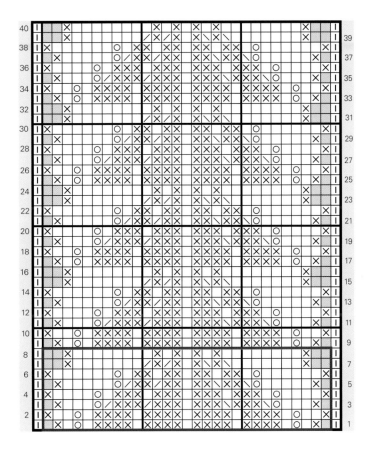

⊞	Knit on RS, knit on WS
□	Knit on RS, purl on WS
⊠	Purl on RS, knit on WS
↘	Sl 1, k1, psso
↗	K2tog
⊙	Yo
▨	No stitch

NO. 21 FLOWERS

For this sample, I cast on 42 stitches. The chart shows 1½ repeats across and 2 in length. One repeat consists of 16 stitches and 20 rows. This is one of the patterns appearing on the Lace Bonanza Tunic on page 145.

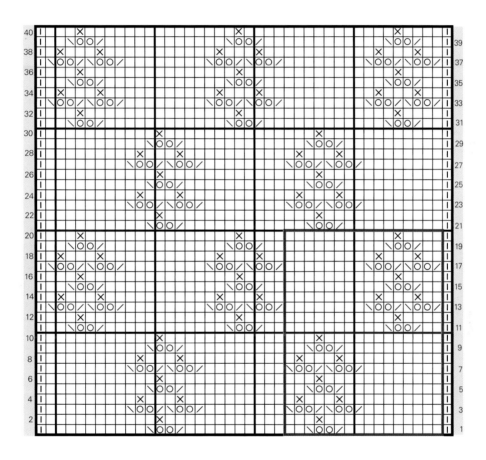

		Knit on RS, knit on WS
		Knit on RS, purl on WS
☒		Purl on RS, knit on WS
⟍		Sl 1, k1, psso
⟋		K2tog
○		Yo

NO. 22 HEART

I cast on 38 stitches for this sample. The chart shows 1 repeat of the heart motif on a stockinette / stocking stitch background. One repeat is 21 stitches and 28 rows. This pattern is used on the Children's Sweater with Hearts (see page 117).

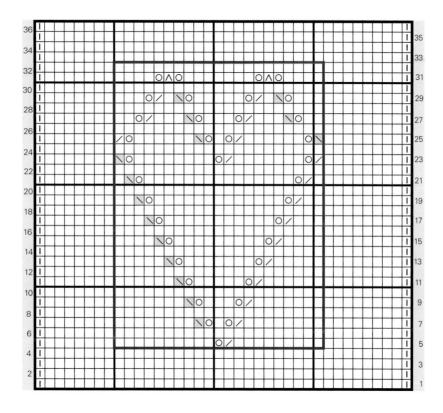

		Knit on RS, knit on WS
		Knit on RS, purl on WS
⃟		Ssk
⃞		K2tog
⃝		Yo
⃤		CDD

NO. 23 HEART ON HEART

This sample begins with 30 stitches cast on. The chart shows 1 repeat of the motif on a stockinette / stocking stitch background. One repeat has 18 stitches and 48 rows. See page 117 for the Children's Sweater with Hearts—this pattern appears on its sleeves.

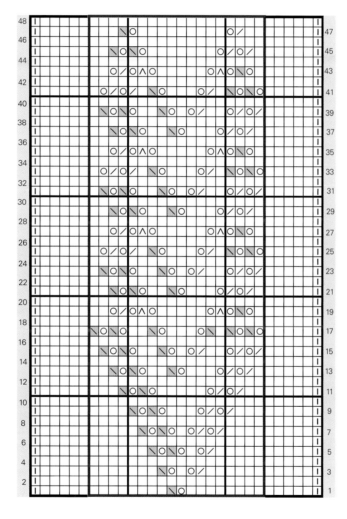

□	Knit on RS, knit on WS
□	Knit on RS, purl on WS
◹	Ssk
◿	K2tog
⊙	Yo
⋀	CDD

Overall Patterns

The patterns in this section are particularly effective as repeats over larger surfaces such as coverlets and entire garments.

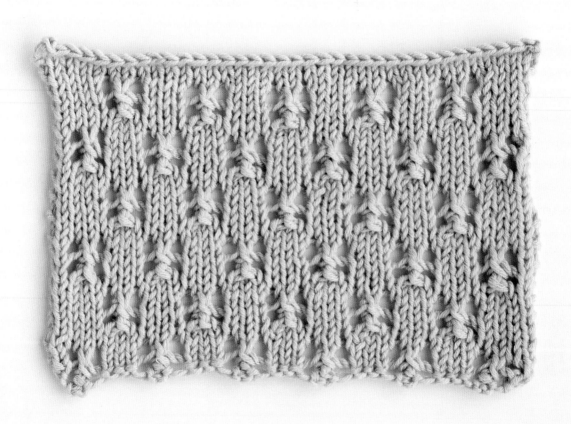

NO. 24 BEE SWARM

I cast on 35 stitches for this sample. The chart shows 5½ repeats across and 3 in length. One repeat has 6 stitches and 12 rows. The Baby Onesie on page 169 is covered with this Bee motif.

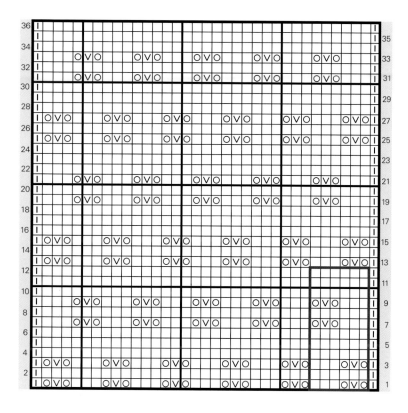

	Knit on RS, knit on WS
	Knit on RS, purl on WS
O	Yarnover
V	Sl 1, k2tog, psso

NO. 25 DIAMOND SYRUP COOKIES

I cast on 51 stitches for this sample. The chart shows 2 complete repeats and a half repeat on each side; there are 2 repeats in length on the chart. One repeat consists of 16 stitches and 24 rows. This motif is repeated all over the pillow cover on page 131.

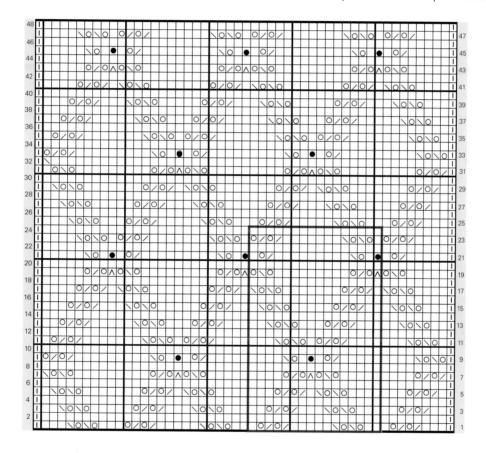

▯	Knit on RS, knit on WS
☐	Knit on RS, purl on WS
◹	Sl 1, k1, psso
◿	K2tog
◉	Yo
●	Knit 5 sts into same st by alternately knitting into front and back of st. Turn and p5; turn and k5tog.

NO. 26 CRYSTAL CHANDELIER

I began this swatch by casting on 42 stitches. The chart shows 3 repeats in length and 4 repeats across, with a divided repeat on each side. One repeat is 8 sts and 16 rows. See this lovely motif on the Hat, Scarf, and Mitten set (page 173).

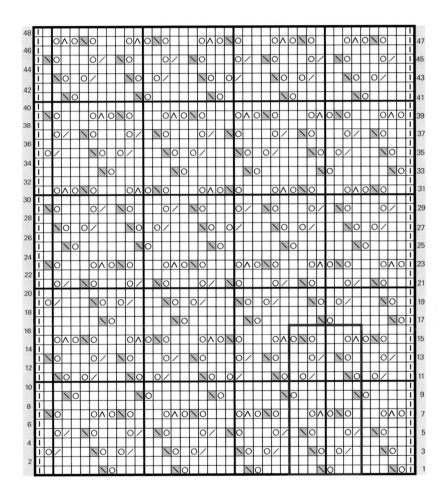

☐ (I)	Knit on RS, knit on WS
☐	Knit on RS, purl on WS
◲	Ssk
◪	K2tog
⊙	Yo
△	CDD

NO. 27 LILY LEAF

I cast on 35 stitches for this swatch. The chart shows 2 repeats across and 1 repeat in length. Each repeat has 16 stitches and 32 rows. See this pattern on the Green Baby Blanket on page 127.

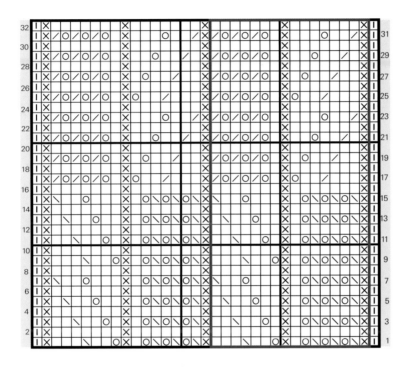

☐ (I)	Knit on RS, knit on WS
☐	Knit on RS, purl on WS
☒	Purl on RS, knit on WS
◺	Sl 1, k1, psso
◹	K2tog
◙	Yo

NO. 28 LILY OF THE VALLEY

This swatch begins with 42 stitches. The chart shows 5 repeats across and 4 in length. One repeat has 8 stitches and 12 rows. See this pattern adorning the Christening Gown and Hat on page 153.

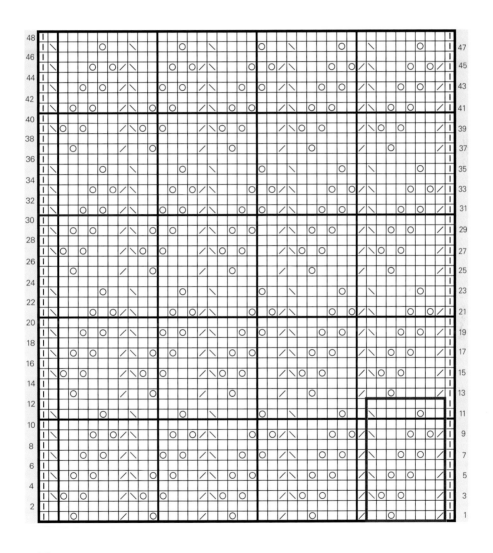

⊡	Knit on RS, knit on WS
□	Knit on RS, purl on WS
⟍	Sl 1, k1, psso
⟋	K2tog
⊙	Yo

NO. 29 GATSBY WAVES

I cast on 46 stitches for this sample. The chart shows 4 repeats across and 2 in length. One repeat has 24 stitches and 24 rows. This pattern is featured on the Bolero with Gatsby Waves on page 149.

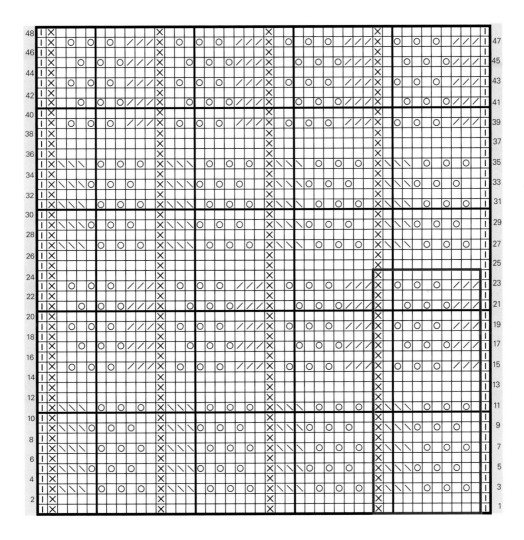

⊡	Knit on RS, knit on WS
☐	Knit on RS, purl on WS
☒	Purl on RS, knit on WS
◺	Sl 1, k1, psso
◿	K2tog
⊙	Yo

NO. 30 WHEAT SPIKE

I cast on 43 stitches for this swatch. The chart shows 4 complete repeats across and 2 in length. One repeat is 8 stitches by 24 rows. There are decreases positioned on each side of the chart; the repeat won't work within the overall stitch count unless these decreases are made. However, if you want to work the pattern in the round, you don't need to worry about these side decreases. The Wheat Spike motif is another of those included on the Lace Bonanza Tunic (see page 145).

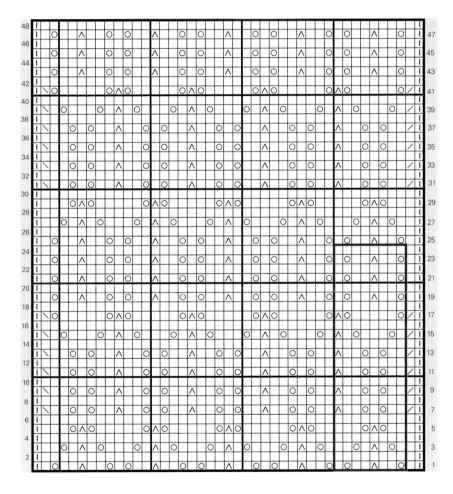

		Knit on RS, knit on WS
□		Knit on RS, purl on WS
⟍		Sl 1, k1, psso
⟋		K2tog
O		Yo
∧		CDD

NO. 31 MEDALLION

For this swatch, I cast on 35 stitches. The chart shows 2 repeats in length and 1 repeat across, with a half repeat on each side. One repeat has 16 stitches and 20 rows. This motif appears on the Yoked Dress (page 107) and the Rugged Sweater with Medallion Pattern (page 157).

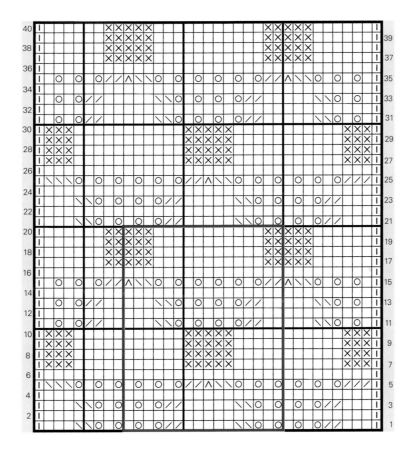

☐	Knit on RS, knit on WS
☐	Knit on RS, purl on WS
☒	Purl on RS, knit on WS
◺	Sl 1, k1, psso
◹	K2tog
◙	Yo
◮	CDD

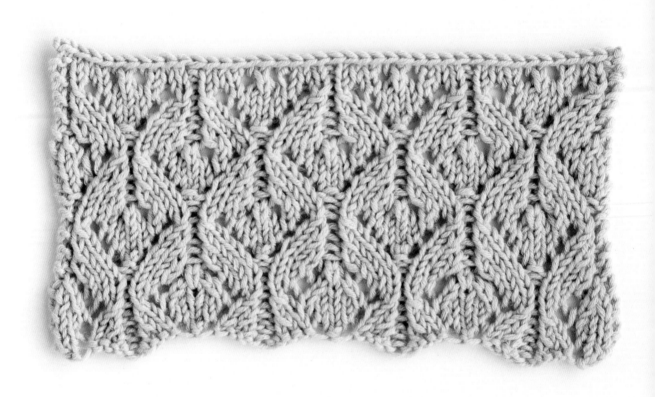

NO. 32 ENFOLDED RIBBONS

I cast on 43 stitches here. The chart shows 2 repeats in length and 3 complete repeats across, with a half repeat at each side. One repeat consists of 10 stitches and 20 rows. This is one of the many motifs on the Lace Bonanza Tunic.

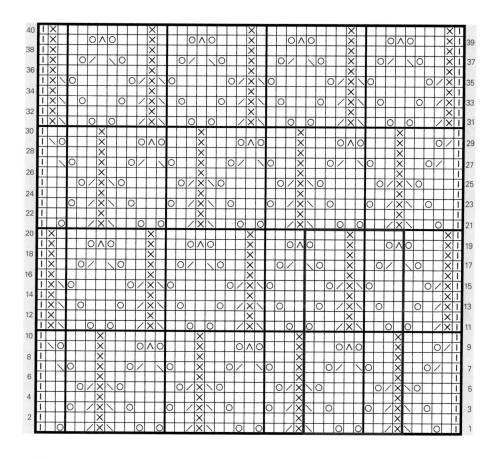

	Knit on RS, knit on WS
	Knit on RS, purl on WS
⊠	Purl on RS, knit on WS
⟍	Sl 1, k1, psso
╱	K2tog
○	Yo
⋀	CDD

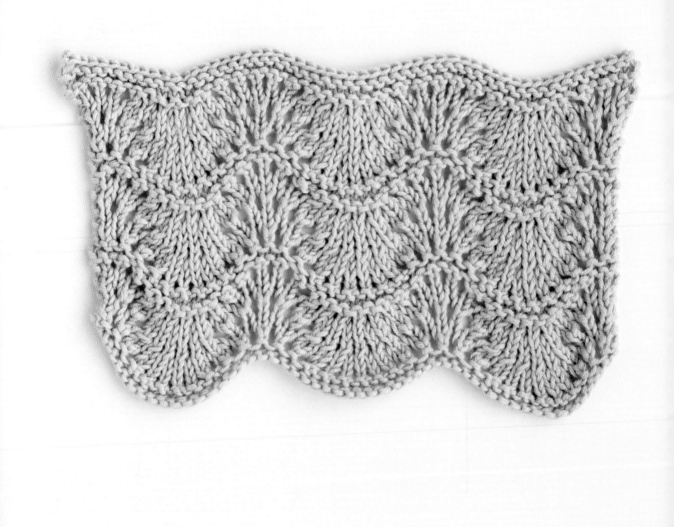

NO. 33 SEA FOAM

I cast on 36 stitches. The chart shows 2 repeats across and 3 in length, ending with 2 rows of garter stitch (knit on both right and wrong sides). One repeat is 17 stitches by 12 rows. You'll find this pattern included on the Lace Bonanza Tunic (see page 145).

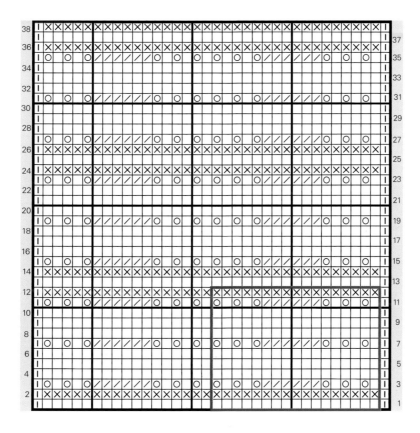

	Knit on RS, knit on WS
	Knit on RS, purl on WS
⊠	Purl on RS, knit on WS
⁄	K2tog
⊙	Yo

NO. 34 SCALLOPS

I cast on 39 stitches for this swatch. The chart shows 2 repeats across (+ 1 stitch) and 2½ repeats in length. One repeat is 18 stitches and 16 rows. The motif covers the lower half of the Lace Top with Scallop Motifs (see page 135).

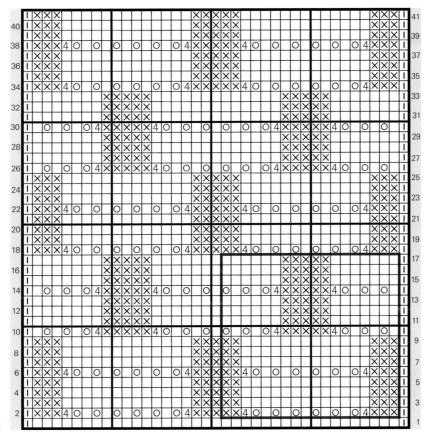

Row 1 = WS

	Knit on RS, knit on WS
	Knit on RS, purl on WS
☒	Purl on RS, knit on WS
⊙	Yo
4	K4tog

Reversible Lace

This group of designs is linked by having lace worked on both the right and wrong sides, which might be tricky. It's a particular challenge if you knit the pattern back and forth, so you'll need to concentrate! The difficulty will be reduced if you work in the round on a circular needle, as I've done for the Dress with Lace Cables on page 101 and the Bluebell Hat on page 99, because you'll always have the right side facing you.

NO. 35 FLAME

I cast on 40 stitches for this sample. The chart shows 4 repeats across and 2 in length. One repeat has 9 stitches and 24 rows. This pattern appears on the Dress for Small Girls (see page 121).

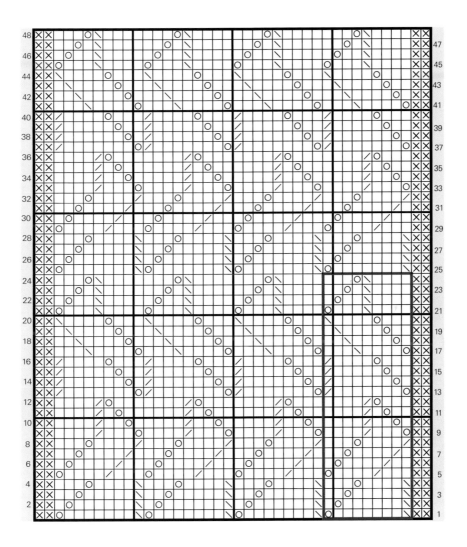

- ☐ Knit on RS, purl on WS
- ☒ Purl on RS, knit on WS
- ◲ On RS: sl 1, k1, psso; on WS: p2tog tbl
- ◱ K2tog on RS, p2tog on WS
- ◉ Yo on RS and WS

NO. 36 SAILOR'S COMFORT

For this swatch, I cast on 39 stitches. The chart shows 2 repeats across (+ 1 stitch) and 10 in length. One repeat has 18 stitches and 4 rows. See page 99 for how it looks on the Bluebell Hat.

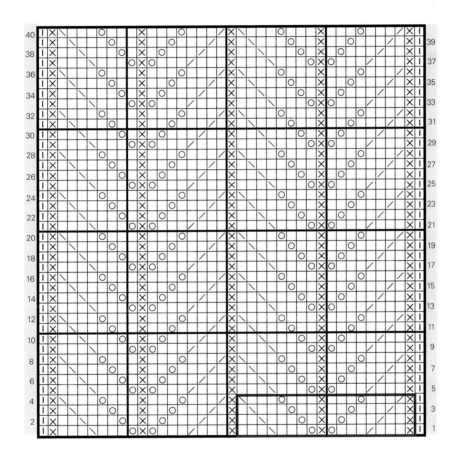

	Knit on RS, knit on WS
	Knit on RS, purl on WS
☒	Purl on RS, knit on WS
⟍	On RS: sl 1, k1, psso; on WS: p2tog tbl
⟋	K2tog on RS, p2tog on WS
⊙	Yo on RS and WS

NO. 37 LACE CABLES

I cast on 44 stitches for this sample. The chart shows 8 rows in length and 3 repeats across with 2 stitches in reverse stockinette / stocking stitch between each repeat. One repeat has 12 stitches and 5 rows. This pattern covers most of the Dress with Lace Cables on page 101.

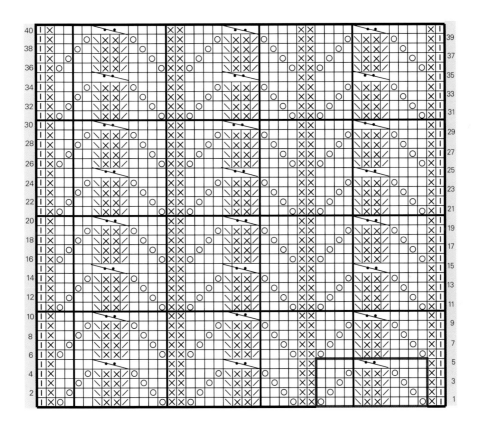

		Knit on RS, knit on WS
		Knit on RS, purl on WS
⊠		Purl on RS, knit on WS
⊡		Yo on both RS and WS
◺		On RS: sl 1, k1, psso; on WS: p2tog tbl
◹		K2tog on RS, p2tog on WS
		On RS: Sl 1 knit st and 2 purl sts onto cable needle and hold in front of work, k1, slip the 2 purl sts on cable needle onto left needle and p2, k1 with last st on cable needle On WS: Sl 1 purl st and 2 knit sts onto cable needle and hold behind work, p1, slip the 2 knit sts on cable needle onto left needle and k2, p1 with last st on cable needle

Twisted Stitch Patterns

The common challenge for the patterns in this section is working twisted knit and purl stitches in addition to the lace.

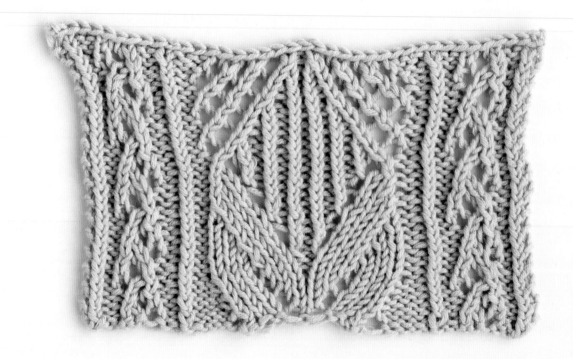

NO. 38 ANGEL WINGS

I cast on 39 stitches for this swatch. The chart shows a complete repeat, which has 28 stitches across and ends with a repeat of the first 9 stitches, plus 1 garter stitch (knit on all rows). One repeat is 32 rows. This pattern is worked all over the Pink Baby Blanket on page 125.

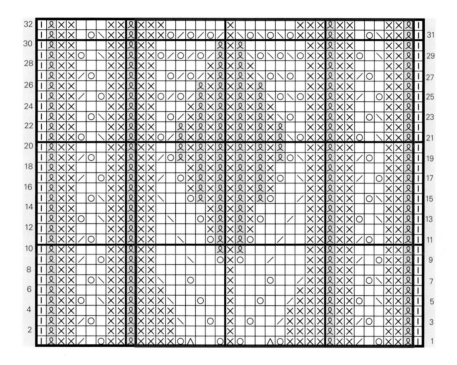

		Knit on RS, knit on WS
		Knit on RS, purl on WS
⊠		Purl on RS, knit on WS
႙		Twisted knit (k1tbl) on RS, twisted purl (p1tbl) on WS
⟍		Sl 1, k1, psso
⟋		K2tog
⊙		Yo
⋀		CDD

NO. 39 SHELL PATTERN

I cast on 44 stitches for this sample. The chart shows 3 repeats across and 1 repeat in length. One repeat has 14 stitches and 50 rows. The Socks with Shell Patterns showcase this motif (see page 141).

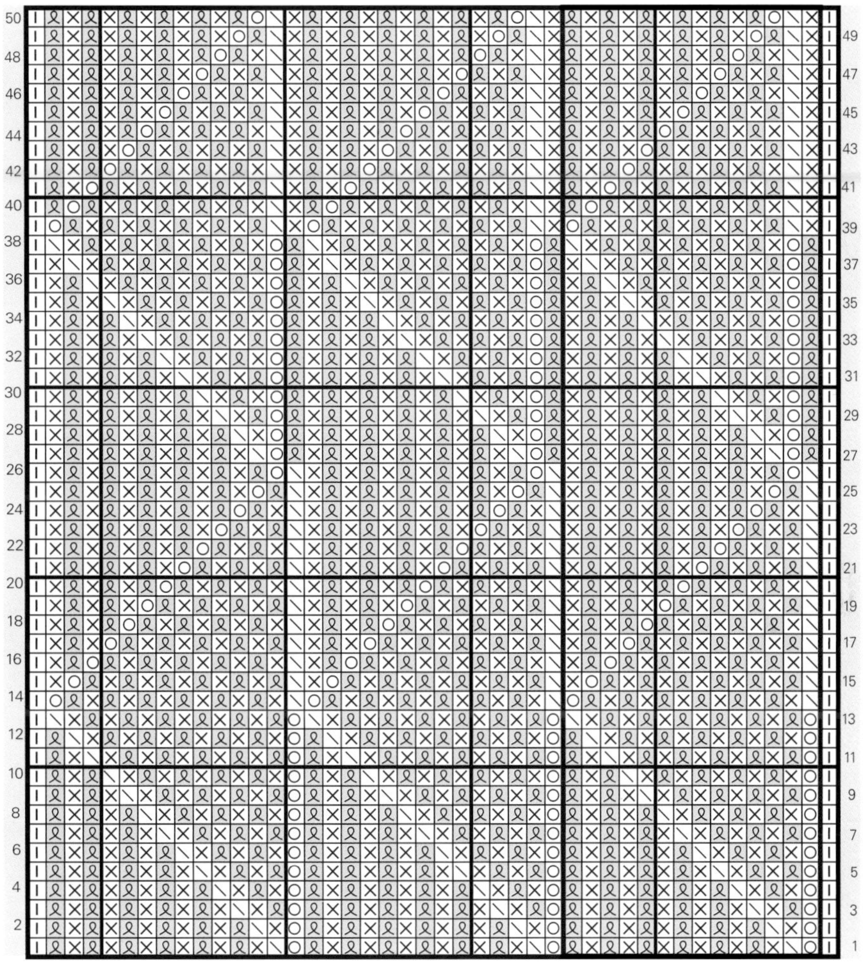

	Knit on RS, knit on WS
Ջ	Twisted knit (k1tbl) on RS, twisted purl (p1tbl) on WS
⊠	Purl on RS, knit on WS
⧄	On RS: Sl 1, k1, psso; on WS, p2tog tbl
⃝	Yo on both RS and WS

NO. 40 PARISIAN PASTRIES

I cast on 49 stitches. The chart shows 2 repeats across, with 1 purl between each repeat, and 6 repeats in length. One repeat has 23 stitches and 6 rows. See the lovely Gloves with this motif on page 165.

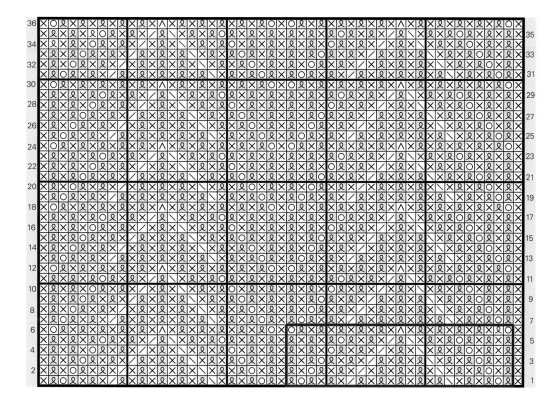

�	Twisted knit (k1tbl) on RS, twisted purl (p1tbl) on WS
✕	Purl on RS, knit on WS
◹	K2tog tbl on RS, p2tog tbl on WS
◺	K2tog on RS, p2tog on WS
◯	Yo on both RS and WS
◭	Turn work so RS faces you, slip 3 sts from right needle to left needle. CDD (slip 2 sts knitwise at same time, k1, psso). Slip new st back on left needle and turn so WS faces you.

GARMENTS, ACCESSORIES AND HOUSEHOLD TEXTILES

PART 2

On the following pages, you'll find patterns for various pieces made with the pattern motifs featured in Part 1. The first items in this section are small so they will be relatively easy to knit. Some of the larger items combine several lace patterns. After you become comfortable with lace knitting, you can also combine patterns for your own designs.

WASHCLOTH AND HAND TOWEL

Here are a couple of easy projects to start with while you learn how to work lace knitting. I grew up with a grandmother who showered the whole family with hand-knitted washcloths and hand towels. When my grandmother died, my mother carried on the tradition, and now I'm the one knitting everyone washcloths and hand towels. Besides being useful in the kitchen and bath at the summer cottage or at home, they also make lovely hostess gifts or presents for new parents.

WASHCLOTH

SKILL LEVEL
Intermediate

FINISHED MEASUREMENTS
Approx. $11\frac{3}{4}$ x 11 in / 30 x 28 cm after blocking

MATERIALS
Yarn:
CYCA #1 (fingering) Mandarin Petit from Sandnes Garn (100% cotton, 195 yd/ 178 m / 50 g)
Yarn Color and Amount:
Dusty Petroleum 6822: 50 g
Needles: U. S. size 2.5 / 3 mm

KNITTING GAUGE
26 sts in pattern = 4 in / 10 cm.
Adjust needle size to obtain correct gauge if necessary.
Crochet Hook: U. S. size B-1 or C-2 / 2.5 mm
Crochet Techniques: Chain st (ch) and single crochet (sc)/UK double crochet (dc)
Edge Sts: Sl the first st purlwise with yarn held in front; knit last st through back loop.

CO 78 sts. Set up pattern: 1 edge st, work charted pattern 9 times, and end with 4 sts in St st (= knit on RS and purl on WS), 1 edge st. Work as

est until piece measures 11 in / 28 cm. BO on RS but do not cut yarn. With crochet hook, sc/UK dc around outer edge, ending with a hanging loop in the top left corner: Ch 14, attach loop with 1 sl st in first ch. Cut yarn and fasten off.

HAND TOWEL

FINISHED MEASUREMENTS
Approx. 19 x $21\frac{1}{4}$ in / 48.5 x 54 cm after blocking

MATERIALS
Yarn:
CYCA #1 (fingering) Mandarin Petit from Sandnes Garn (100% cotton, 195 yd/ 178 m / 50 g)
Yarn Color and Amount:
Dusty Petroleum 6822: 150 g
Needles: U. S. size 2.5 / 3 mm

KNITTING GAUGE
26 sts in pattern = 4 in / 10 cm.
Adjust needle size to obtain correct gauge if necessary.
Crochet Hook: U. S. size B-1 or C-2 / 2.5 mm
Crochet Techniques: Chain st (ch) and single crochet (sc)
Edge Sts: Sl the first st purlwise with yarn held in front; knit last st through back loop.

CO 126 sts. Set up pattern: 1 edge st, work charted pattern 15 times, and end with 4 sts in St st (= knit on RS and purl on WS), 1 edge st. Work as est until piece measures $21\frac{1}{4}$ in / 54 cm. BO on RS but do not cut yarn. With crochet hook, sc/UK dc around outer edge, ending with a hanging loop in the top left corner: Ch 14, attach loop with 1 sl st in first ch. Cut yarn and fasten off.

☐   Knit on RS, purl on WS

☒   Purl on RS, knit on WS

◺   Sl 1, k1, psso

◿   K2tog

◎   Yo

BLUEBELL HAT

The pattern for this hat creates a wavy bell-like edging along the cast-on edge, hence the name "bluebell." Our version is knitted with a pretty baby alpaca and silk yarn for a warm, lightweight hat.

SKILL LEVEL
Intermediate

SIZE
One size, child

MATERIALS
Yarn:
CYCA #2 (sport, baby) BabySilk from Du Store Alpakka (50% silk, 50% alpaca, 145 yd/ 133 m / 50 g)
Yarn Color and Amount:
Lilac 338: 50 g
Needles: U. S. size 4 / 3.5 mm: 16 in / 40 cm circular and set of 5 dpn

GAUGE
26 sts in pattern = 4 in / 10 cm; 22 sts in stockinette / stocking stitch = 4 in / 10 cm.
Adjust needle size to obtain correct gauge if necessary.

With circular, CO 108 sts. Join, being careful not to twist cast-on row; pm for beginning of rnd. Work 10 repeats up in pattern following the chart. Now change to St st and shape top. When sts no longer fit around circular, change to dpn.

Rnd 1: (K7, k2tog) around = 96 sts rem.
Rnd 2: Knit around.
Rnd 3: (K6, k2tog) around = 84 sts rem.
Rnd 4: Knit around.
Rnd 5: (K5, k2tog) around = 72 sts rem.
Rnd 6: Knit around.
Rnd 7: (K4, k2tog) around = 60 sts rem.
Rnd 8: Knit around.
Rnd 9: (K3, k2tog) around = 48 sts rem.
Rnd 10: Knit around.
Rnd 11: (K2, k2tog) around = 36 sts rem.
Rnd 12: Knit around.
Rnd 13: (K1, k2tog) around = 24 sts rem.
Rnd 14: Knit around.
Rnd 15: (K2tog) around = 12 sts rem.

Cut yarn and draw end through rem sts; tighten. Weave in all ends neatly on WS.

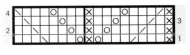

☐ Knit
☒ Purl
◻ Yo
◺ Sl 1, k1, psso
◹ K2tog

Decrease over the
purl sts in each
section (see text)

Pattern
repeat

☐ Knit

☒ Purl

⊙ Yo

⧄ K2tog

⧅ Sl 1, k1, psso

Sl 1 knit st and 2 purl sts onto
cable needle and hold in front
of work, k1, slip the 2 purl sts on
cable needle onto left needle
and p2, k1 with last st on cable
needle.

DRESS WITH LACE CABLES

This design's look is classic and can be varied by using different colors and yarn. Here, we've knitted it in summery white—perfect for a flowergirl or bridesmaid. Knit it in another color for a pretty everyday dress.

SKILL LEVEL
Intermediate

SIZES
1 (2, 3, 4) years

FINISHED MEASUREMENTS
Chest: $17\frac{3}{4}$ ($19\frac{3}{4}$, $21\frac{3}{4}$, $23\frac{3}{4}$) in / 45 (50, 55, 60) cm
Total Length: $17\frac{3}{4}$ (19, 20, $21\frac{3}{4}$) in / 45 (48, 51, 55) cm

MATERIALS
Yarn:
CYCA #2 (sport, baby) Bjork from Viking of Norway (90% cotton, 10% Merino wool, 164 yd/105 m / 50 g)
Yarn Color and Amount:
White 500: 150 (150, 200, 200) g
Needles: U. S. size 4 / 3.5 mm: 16 in / 40 cm circular or long circular for magic loop; cable needle
Other Materials: approx. $49\frac{1}{4}$ in / 125 cm silk ribbon

KNITTING GAUGE
25 sts in pattern = 4 in / 10 cm; 24 sts in stockinette / stocking stitch = 4 in / 10 cm.
Adjust needle size to obtain correct gauge if necessary.
Crochet Hook: U. S. size D-3 / 3 mm
Crochet Techniques: Single crochet (sc)/UK double crochet (dc), slip stitch (sl st), and crab stitch (sc/UK dc worked left to right)

Skirt
The skirt is composed of 9 (10, 11, 12) panels with 22 pattern sts each. CO 198 (220, 242, 264) sts. Join, being careful not to twist cast-on row; pm for beginning of rnd. Work in pattern following the chart until piece measures 2 in / 5 cm. Now decrease 18 (20, 22, 24) sts by working p2tog at the beginning and end of each purl st panel = 180 (200, 220, 240) sts rem. Decrease the same way on the purl panels every 2 in / 5 cm until 126 (140, 154, 168) sts rem. Continue in pattern until skirt measures $12\frac{3}{4}$ ($13\frac{1}{2}$, $14\frac{1}{4}$, 15) in / 32 (34, 36, 38) cm. Now p2tog over all the purl sts and the 2 center sts in the pattern rep (above the cable) = 108 (120, 132, 144) sts rem. Knit 4 rnds in St st.

Eyelet Panel
Rnd 1: Purl.
Rnd 2: (Yo, k2tog) around.
Rnd 3: Purl.
Rnds 4-7: Knit.
Divide piece for front and back with 54 (60, 66, 72) sts each.

Back
Shape armholes by binding off 1 st at the beginning of each row a total of 8 times = 46 (52, 58, 64) sts rem. When piece measures $3\frac{1}{2}$ (4, $4\frac{1}{4}$, $4\frac{3}{4}$) in / 9 (10, 11, 12) cm from the eyelet rnd, bind off the center 22 (24, 26, 28) sts

for the back neck and work each side separately. Decrease another 1-1 sts at neck edge (on every other row) = 10 (12, 14, 16) sts rem for shoulder. When piece measures $17\frac{3}{4}$ (19, 20, $21\frac{3}{4}$) in / 45 (48, 51, 55) cm, BO. Work second shoulder the same way, reversing shaping to correspond.

Front
Work as for back until piece measures $2\frac{1}{2}$ in / 6 cm from eyelet rnd. BO the center 12 (14, 16, 18) sts for neck and work each side separately. BO another 1-1 sts at neck edge (on every other row) = 10 (12, 14, 16) sts rem for shoulder. When piece measures $17\frac{3}{4}$ (19, 20, $21\frac{3}{4}$) in / 45 (48, 51, 55) cm, BO. Work second shoulder the same way, reversing shaping to correspond.

Finishing
Join shoulders.

Neck and Armhole Edgings
Around neck and each armhole: With crochet hook, work 1 rnd sc/UK dc around. Join with 1 sl st into 1st sc/UK dc. Work 1 rnd crab st and join with 1 sl st into 1st sc/UK dc. Cut yarn and fasten off.

Weave in all ends neatly on WS. Beginning at center front, thread the ribbon through the eyelet rnd and tie into a bow at front.

SWEATER WITH LEAFY VINES

It's wonderful to walk barefoot on the beach, but once the sun has set, it's good to have a nice light sweater to wear. The yarn I used is a blend of cotton and bamboo for an extra soft garment. The charts are on page 104.

SKILL LEVEL
Experienced

SIZES
XS (S, M, L, XL, XXL)

FINISHED MEASUREMENTS
Chest: 32¼ (36, 37½, 39½, 43, 46½) in / 82 (91, 95, 100, 109, 118) cm
Total Length: 22¾ (23¾, 24½, 25¼, 26, 26¾) in / 58 (60, 62, 64, 66, 68) cm

MATERIALS
Yarn:
CYCA #3 (DK, light worsted) Bamboo from Viking of Norway (50% cotton, 50% bamboo rayon, 120 yd/110 m / 50 g)

Yarn Color and Amount:
Blue-Green 628: 450 (500, 550, 550, 600, 650) g

Needles: U. S. size 4 / 3.5 mm: 32 or 40 in / 80 or 100 cm circular; set of 5 dpn

KNITTING GAUGE
22 sts in pattern and stockinette / stocking stitch = 4 in / 10 cm. Adjust needle size to obtain correct gauge if necessary.

Crochet Hook: U. S. size D-3 / 3 mm

Crochet Techniques: Single crochet (sc)/UK double crochet (dc), slip stitch (sl st), and crab stitch (sc/UK dc worked left to right)

Body
With circular, CO 181 (201, 210, 221, 241, 261) sts. Join, being careful not to twist cast-on row; pm for beginning of rnd. Work 2 rnds garter st = knit 1 rnd, purl 1 rnd.
Pm at each side with 90 (100, 105, 110, 120, 130) sts for back and 91 (101, 105, 111, 121, 131) sts for front. Set up pattern—front: p30 (35, 37, 40, 45, 50), pattern following Chart 1, p30 (35, 37, 40, 45, 50); back: knit. Continue as est until piece measures 15 (15¾, 16¼, 16½, 17, 17¼) in / 38 (40, 41, 42, 43, 44) cm. Divide for back and front and work each separately.

Back
For all sizes: BO 3-2-1-1-1-1 sts at each side to shape armholes = 72 (82, 87, 92, 102, 112) sts rem. Continue without further shaping until piece measures 22 (22¾ (23¾, 24½, 25¼, 26) in / 56 (58, 60, 62, 64, 66) cm. BO the center 22 (32, 33, 38, 44, 54) sts for back neck and work each side separately. Now BO 2-2-1 sts at neck edge = 20 20, 22, 22, 24, 24) sts rem for shoulder. BO rem sts. Work the other side, reversing shaping to correspond.

Front
Shape armholes at each side as for back. After completing decreases, divide the piece with 37 (42, 44, 47, 52, 57) sts for left front and 36 (41, 43, 46, 51, 56) sts for right front. Work each side separately. Make a note of where you end in the pattern on Chart 1.

Right Front
Pick up and knit 1 st = 37 (42, 44, 47, 52, 57) sts.
Continue as follows:
RS: Work Chart 3 (16 sts), purl to end of row.
NOTE: Chart 3 is an extension of Chart 1, so make sure the pattern matches by counting up to the right row on the chart.
WS: Knit until 2 sts rem before Chart 3, k2tog, work Chart 3.
Rep these two rows until 20 (20, 22, 22, 24, 24) sts rem for shoulder. Continue until front is same length as back. BO on RS.

Left Front
= 37 (42, 44, 47, 52, 57) sts
RS: Purl to pattern and then work Chart 2 (16 sts).
WS: Work Chart 2, k2tog, tbl, knit to end of row.
NOTE: Chart 2 is an extension of Chart 1, so make sure the pattern

matches by counting up to the right row on the chart.

Rep these two rows until 20 (20, 22, 22, 24, 24) sts rem for shoulder. Continue until front is same length as back. BO on RS.

Sleeves
With dpn, CO 41 (43, 45, 47, 49, 51) sts. Join and pm for beginning of rnd = center of underarm. Set up pattern: P14 (15, 16, 17, 18, 19), work pattern following Chart 4 (13 sts), p14 (15, 16, 17, 18, 19). Work as est, increasing 1

st on each side of underarm marker on every 6th rnd to shape sleeve until sleeve is 17¼ (17¼, 17¾, 17¾, 18¼, 18¼) in / 44 (44, 45, 45, 46, 46) cm long or desired length.
Now begin working back and forth. For all sizes, BO 3-2-1-1-1-1 sts at each side to shape sleeve cap. BO rem sts. Make the second sleeve the same way, *except* begin the rep on Row 9 of Chart 4 for the right sleeve.

Finishing
Join shoulders and attach sleeves.

Edging Around V-Neck
Beginning at center front, work 1 sc/ UK dc in each st around neck. End with 1 sl st into 1st sc/UK dc. Work 1 rnd crab st, ending with 1 sl st into first crab st. Cut yarn and fasten off.

Edging Around Lower Edges of Body and Sleeves
Beginning at side of body or center of underarm on sleeves, work 1 sc/UK dc in each st around. End with 1 sl st into 1st sc/UK dc. Work 1 rnd crab st, ending with 1 sl st into first crab st. Cut yarn and fasten off.

Chart 1

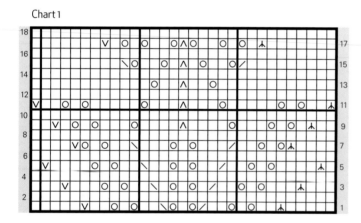

Chart 4—Sleeves

← Begin here for right sleeve

← Begin here for left sleeve

13 sts

Chart 2—Right Front

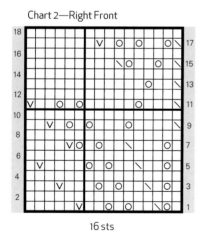

16 sts

Chart 3—Left Front

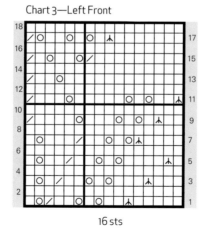

16 sts

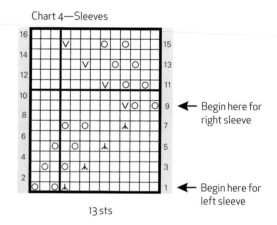

☐ Knit on RS, purl on WS

◪ Sl 1, k1, psso

◪ K2tog

◙ Yo

◹ Sl 1, k2tog, psso

⋏ K3tog

⋀ CDD

YOKED DRESS

I knitted this dress with a wonderful cotton and cashmere yarn. The skirt and top are each knitted separately and then sewn together so the pretty waves from the medallion pattern are showcased. The charts are on page 109.

SKILL LEVEL
Experienced

SIZES
S (M, L, XL)

FINISHED MEASUREMENTS
Chest: 31½ (34, 36¼, 38½) in / 80 (86, 92, 98) cm
Circumference at Lower Edge: approx. 53½ (58¼, 63, 67¾) in / 136 (148, 160, 172) cm
Total Length: 34¾ (35½, 36¼, 37) in / 88 (90, 92, 94) cm

MATERIALS
Yarn:
CYCA #2 (sport, baby) Elise from Permin (90% cotton, 10% cashmere, 126 yd/115 m / 25 g)
Yarn Color and Amount:
Jade 881113: 375 (375, 400, 425) g
Needles: U. S. size 2.5 / 3 mm: 32 and 60 in / 80 and 150 cm circular + an extra needle for 3-needle bind-off

KNITTING GAUGE
26 sts in stockinette / stocking stitch = 4 in / 10 cm; 28 sts in pattern = 4 in / 10 cm.
Adjust needle size to obtain correct gauge if necessary.
Crochet Hook: U. S. size B-1 or C-2 / 2.5 mm
Crochet Techniques: Single crochet (sc)/UK double crochet (dc), slip stitch (sl st), and crab stitch (sc/UK dc worked left to right)

Skirt
With longer circular, CO 352 (384, 416, 448) sts. Join, being careful not to twist cast-on row; pm for beginning of rnd. Knit 1 rnd. Now work following Chart 1, which is worked all the way to the yoke. When piece measures 6 in / 15 cm, decrease 22 (24, 26, 28) sts as shown on the chart = 330 (360, 390, 420) sts rem. Decrease 22 (24, 26, 28) sts every 4 in / 10 cm following the chart. When piece measures 21¾ in / 55 cm, decrease 2 sts on each panel = 220 (240, 260, 280) sts rem. Work in pattern over rem sts until skirt measures 22 (22½, 22¾, 23¼) in / 56 (57, 58, 59) cm or desired length. BO loosely.

Yoke
With circular, CO 224 (240, 256, 272) sts. Join, being careful not to twist cast-on row. Pm at each side with 112 (120, 128, 136) sts between each marker. Work in medallion pattern following Chart 2 until yoke is 6¼ in / 16 cm long. Divide work, slipping front sts to a holder.

Back
Continue in pattern following Chart 2, but, *at the same time*, BO 3-2-2-1-1 sts at each side = 94 (102, 110, 118) sts rem. If you can't work a complete repeat at the sides, omit a yarnover/ decrease pair as necessary to maintain a consistent stitch count of 94 (102, 110, 118) sts. When armhole measures 4¾ (5¼, 5½, 6) in / 12 (13, 14, 15) cm, BO the center 22 (26, 30, 34) sts for back neck and work each side separately. BO another 3-2-1-1-1 sts at neck edge (all sizes). When armhole depth is 6¼ (6¾, 7, 7½) in / 16 (17, 18, 19) cm, place rem 28 (30, 32, 34) sts on a holder. Work the other side to match.

Front
Work as for back until armhole depth is 2½ in / 6 cm. BO the center 18 (22, 26, 30) sts for neck and work each side separately. BO another 3-2-1-1-1-1-1 sts. When armhole is same depth as for back, place rem 28 (30, 32, 34) sts on a holder. Work the other side to correspond.

Finishing
Place sts of right front on one gauge-size circular and the sts of right back on a second circular (same size). BO with 3-needle bind-off as follows. Hold the two pieces with RS facing RS. With a third needle, knit the first st of each needle tog. *Knit the next pair of sts together and pass the first st on right needle over the second*. Rep from * to * until all sts have been

Chart 1

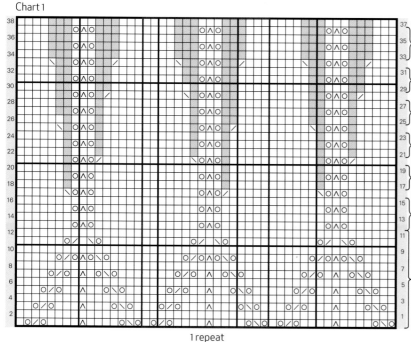

BO on RS
Rep until piece measures 22 (22½, 22¾, 23¼) in / 56 (57, 58, 59) cm

Decrease here when piece measures 21¾ in / 55 cm
Rep until piece measures 21¾ in / 55 cm

Decrease here when piece measures 17¾ in / 45 cm
Rep until piece measures 17¾ in / 45 cm

Decrease here when piece measures 13¾ in / 35 cm
Rep until piece measures 13¾ in / 35 cm

Decrease here when piece measures 9¾ in / 25 cm
Rep until piece measures 9¾ in / 25 cm

Decrease here when piece measures 6 in / 15 cm
Rep until piece measures 6 in / 15 cm

Work this repeat only once

1 repeat

Chart 2

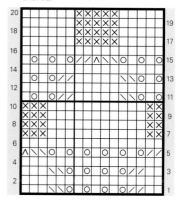

☐ Knit on RS, purl on WS

☒ Purl on RS, knit on WS

⊚ Yo

⧅ Sl 1, k1, psso

⧄ K2tog

⋀ CDD

▨ No stitch

bound off. Fasten off last st. Join left shoulders the same way. Turn skirt inside out and carefully steam press under a damp pressing cloth. Pin the yoke to the skirt with WS facing out. The skirt should be attached about ⅜ in / 1 cm (¾ in / 2 cm at wave peaks) in on the yoke so that the waves point down from yoke.

Use whip stitch to sew the pieces together.

Edgings
Beginning at center of underarm, work 1 rnd sc/UK dc around the right armhole, skipping every 4th st. Then work 1 rnd with 1 crab st in each sc/ UK dc. Join last st to first with 1 sl st.

Work around left armhole the same way.
Edge the neckline with 1 rnd sc/UK dc, beginning at center back. Work 1 rnd with 1 crab st in each sc/ UK dc. Join last st to first sc/ UK dc with 1 sl st. Weave in all ends neatly on WS.

GIRLS' SWEATER WITH LUPINE PATTERN

This sweater was made with mercerized cotton yarn for a lovely smooth surface. If you knit the sweater with a wool or alpaca yarn at the same gauge, it will be even warmer and cozier.

SKILL LEVEL
Experienced

SIZES
2 (4, 6, 8, 10, 12) years

FINISHED MEASUREMENTS
Chest: 24¾ (26¾, 28¼, 30¼, 32, 34) in / 63 (68, 72, 77, 81, 86) cm
Total Length: 14¼ (15½, 16½, 17¾, 19, 20) in / 36 (39, 42, 45, 48, 51) cm
Sleeve Length: 9½ (11, 11¾, 13, 14¼, 15½) in / 24 (28, 30, 33, 36, 39) cm

MATERIALS
Yarn:
CYCA #4 (worsted, afghan, Aran)
Matilda from Svarta Fåret (100% mercerized cotton, 126 yd/115 m / 50 g)

Yarn Color and Amount:
Light Purple 61: 200 (250, 300, 350, 400, 450) g
Needles: U. S. size 6 / 4 mm: circular and set of 5 dpn

KNITTING GAUGE
20 sts in stockinette / stocking stitch = 4 in / 10 cm; 19 sts in pattern = 4 in / 10 cm.
Adjust needle size to obtain correct gauge if necessary.

Crochet Hook: U. S. size E-4 / 3.5 mm
Crochet Techniques: Single crochet (sc)/ UK dc, slip stitch (sl st), and double crochet (dc)/UK treble crochet (tr)

Front and Back
With circular, CO 126 (136, 144, 154, 162, 172) sts. Join, being careful not to twist cast-on row. Pm at each side with 63 (68, 72, 77, 81, 86) sts between markers for front and back. Set up pattern: Work 0 (2, 0, 2, 0, 2) sts in St st, work chart rep 7 (7, 8, 8, 9, 9) times, work 0 (5, 0, 5, 0, 5) sts in St st, work chart rep 7 (7, 8, 8, 9, 9) times, work 0 (3, 0, 3, 0, 3) sts in St st. When piece measures 8¼ (9, 9¾, 11, 11¾, 12¾) in / 21 (23, 25, 28, 30, 32) cm, BO 2 sts at each side of each marker and then work each side separately.

Back
= 59 (64, 68, 73, 77, 82) sts. From this point on, work back and forth in St st. When piece measures 13½ (14½, 15¾, 17, 18¼, 19¼) in / 34 (37, 40, 43, 46, 49) cm, BO the center 13 (16, 16, 19, 21, 22) sts for back neck and work each side separately. BO another 2-1 sts at neck edge. When piece measures 14¼ (15½, 16½, 17¾, 19,

20) in / 36 (39, 42, 45, 48, 51) cm, BO rem sts on RS for shoulder = 20 (21, 23, 24, 25, 27) sts. Work the other side the same way, reversing shaping to correspond.

Front
= 59 (64, 68, 73, 77, 82) sts. Work as for back until piece measures 11¾ (13, 14¼, 15, 16¼, 17¼) in / 30 (33, 36, 38, 41, 44) cm. BO the center 9 (12, 12, 15, 17, 18) sts for neck and work each side separately. BO another 2-2-1 sts at neck edge. When piece measures 14¼ (15½, 16½, 17¾, 19, 20) in / 36 (39, 42, 45, 48, 51) cm, BO rem sts on RS for shoulder = 20 (21, 23, 24, 25, 27) sts. Work the other side the same way, reversing shaping to correspond.

Sleeves
With dpn, CO 36 sts (all sizes). Divide

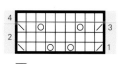

☐ Knit
◫ Sl 1, k1, psso
◪ K2tog
◉ Yo

sts evenly over 4 needles and join. Work in charted pattern 2 times in length. On the next rnd, increase evenly spaced around to 38 (38, 40, 40, 44) sts. Pm at beginning of rnd (= center of underarm) and continue in St st. *At the same time*, shape sleeve by increasing 1 st on each side of marker every ¾ in / 2 cm (all sizes) until there are 60 (62, 68, 68, 72, 74) sts. If necessary, space increases more closely together near top of sleeve. When sleeve is 9½ (11, 11¾, 13, 14¼, 15½) in / 24 (28, 30, 33, 36, 39) cm long, loosely BO all sts.

Finishing
Join shoulders. Attach sleeves.

Neckband
Crochet neckband as follows: 1 sl st, *3 dc/UK tr in next st, skip 1 st, 1 sl st in next st, skip 1 st*; rep * to * around, ending with 1 sl st. Make sure the neckband doesn't draw in or ruffle. Cut yarn and weave in all ends neatly on WS. Block sweater by laying on a damp towel, patting out to finished measurements, and covering with another damp towel. Leave until completely dry.

ZIGZAG SHAWL

I've used various shades of this semi-solid yarn, and each color combination I try always seems even prettier than the last. I began this shawl by knitting the two borders in the Waves on the Beach pattern, and then picked up and knitted stitches along one edge to knit the main body of the shawl in the Zigzag pattern. The second border is sewn on with finishing.

SKILL LEVEL
Experienced

SIZE
One size

FINISHED MEASUREMENTS
Approx. 24½ x 56¾ in / 62 x 144 cm

MATERIALS
Yarn:
CYCA #1 (light fingering) Silk Blend Fino from Manos del Uruguay (70% Merino wool, 30% silk, 490 yd/ 448 m / 100 g)
Yarn Color and Amount:
Abalone 3301: 200 g
Needles: U. S. size 2.5 / 3 mm

GAUGE
Approx. 22 sts in lace pattern = 4 in / 10 cm.
Adjust needle size to obtain correct gauge if necessary.

Border
CO 12 sts and work border following Chart 1. Rep until you have 8 points. If you are in the center of a repeat and must cast on from the work, I recommend that you write down where you began in the pattern. It's not always easy to see where you are on a chart. BO.

Make one more border and block both, pinning out well. See the sketch on page 163. Dampen well and leave until dry.

Shawl
With wrong side facing, pick up 132 sts along straight edge of a border, skipping every 4th or 5th st to get the right stitch count. Now work following Chart 2 until piece measures approx. 54 in / 137 cm, including border. BO. Place second border RS facing RS along bound-off edge of shawl. Whip stitch the pieces together in the outermost stitch loop on each piece.

Finishing
Weave in all ends neatly on WS. Block the shawl, pinning long sides so as to emphasize the waves in the pattern. Dampen well and leave until completely dry.

Chart 1

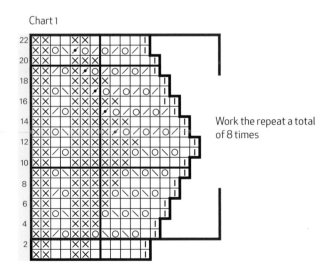

Work the repeat a total of 8 times

Chart 2

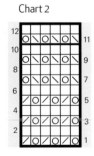

	Knit on RS, knit on WS
	Knit on RS, purl on WS
☒	Purl on RS, knit on WS
◺	Sl 1, k1, psso
◿	K2tog
◯	Yo
◿	P2tog

CHILDREN'S SWEATER WITH HEARTS

A sweater with hearts that's full of charm. This version was knitted with a soft and very pretty cotton yarn, available in more than 30 colors. Choose your favorite color and knit one for your own little sweetheart! The charts are on page 118.

SKILL LEVEL
Experienced

SIZES
1-2 (3-4, 6, 8, 10, 12) years

FINISHED MEASUREMENTS
Chest: 23¾ (24½, 26, 28¼, 29¼, 31½) in / 60 (62, 66, 72, 74, 80) cm
Total Length: 13½ (15, 18¼, 19¾, 21¼, 22) in / 34 (38, 46, 50, 54, 56) cm
Sleeve Length: 8¾ (9½, 11, 11¾, 13½, 15) in / 22 (24, 28, 30, 34, 38) cm

MATERIALS
Yarn:
CYCA #1 (fingering) Mandarin Petit from Sandnes Garn (100% cotton, 195 yd/ 178 m / 50 g)
Yarn Color and Amount:
Purple 5553: 150 (150, 200, 200, 200, 250) g
Needles: U. S. size 2.5 / 3 mm: circular and set of 5 dpn
Other Materials: 1 button

KNITTING GAUGE
27 sts in stockinette / stocking stitch = 4 in / 10 cm.
Adjust needle size to obtain correct gauge if necessary.
Crochet Hook: U. S. size B-1 or C-2 / 2.5 mm
Crochet Techniques: Chain st (ch) and slip st (sl st)
NOTES: For edge sts, always knit the first and last stitch on all rows, unless otherwise specified. Read through the pattern completely before you start knitting, as several steps are worked simultaneously.

Front and Back
With circular, CO 162 (168, 178, 194, 200, 216) sts. Working back and forth, work 6 rows St st (don't forget edge sts). Next, work eyelet row: (k2tog, yo) across. Take all measurements from this row.
Now work in St st until piece measures 8¼ (9½, 10¾, 11¾, 13, 14¼) in / 21 (24, 27, 30, 33, 36) cm, ending with a WS row.
Shape armholes: K34 (36, 38, 42, 44, 48), BO 12 sts, k70 (72, 78, 86, 88, 96), BO 12, k34 (36, 38, 42, 44, 48). Set body aside while you make the sleeves.

Sleeves
With dpn, CO 44 (46, 48, 50, 52, 52) sts. Divide sts onto dpn and join. Knit 6 rnds. Next, work eyelet rnd: (k2tog, yo) around. Take all measurements from this row. Pm around the first and last sts of rnd. Shape sleeves by increasing 1 st on each side of the 2 center underarm sts on every 6th rnd until there are a total of 64 (72, 72, 80, 88, 88) sts. If necessary, space increases more closely together towards top of sleeve. *At the same time*, when sleeve measures 1¼ (2, 3½, 4¼, 6, 7½) in / 3 (5, 9, 11, 15, 19) cm, work pattern following Chart 1. Make sure the pattern is centered on the sleeve. When sleeve is 8¾ (9½, 11, 11¾, 13½, 15) in / 22 (24, 28, 30, 34, 38) cm long, BO the center 12 sts at underarm. Set 1st sleeve aside while you make the second sleeve the same way.

Raglan Shaping
Place the sleeves on the circular over the bound-off underarm sts on body = 242 (264, 274, 306, 328, 344) sts total. Pm at each junction of sleeve and body. Decrease for raglan shaping as follows: K2tog tbl before marker and k2tog after marker. Decrease at all 4 markers = total of 8 sts decreased per row. Decrease the same way every RS rows = every other row. *At the same time* as working raglan shaping, when work measures 9 (10¾, 13¾, 15½, 17, 17¾) in / 23 (27, 35, 39, 43, 45) cm, work from Chart 2 over the back. Count to the center stitch of the

Chart 2

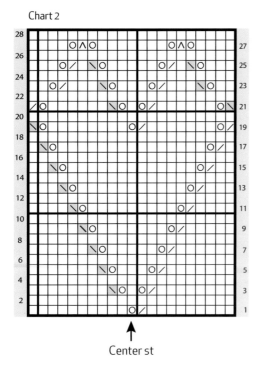

Center st

Chart 1

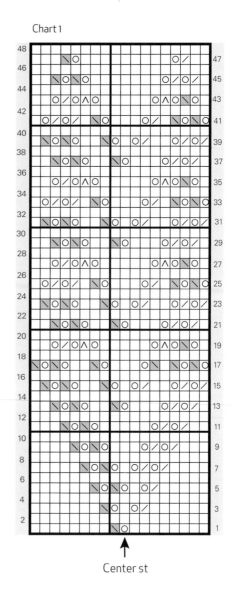

Center st

	Knit on RS, purl on WS
	Ssk
	K2tog
	Yo
	CDD

back so you can center the charted pattern.

When piece measures 13½ (15, 18¼, 19¾, 21¼, 22) in / 34 (38, 46, 50, 54, 56) cm, finish with an I-cord bind-off. CO 2 sts at beginning of row, *k1, k2tog tbl with next 2 sts (1 from cord, 1 from body), slip last 2 sts back on left needle*; rep * to * across, binding off last 2 sts the usual way.

Front Edgings
Beginning at bottom of right front, work a crochet edging with 1 sl st in

each st inside edge st, up until 3/8 in / 1 cm below front neck. Ch 6-8 sts for the button loop (depending on button size), skip 6-8 sts and attach ch with 1 sl st into 1st st of neckband. Work sl st up the left front the same way, omitting button loop.

Finishing
Fold hem along eyelet row of body and sew cast-on edge down on WS with whip stitch. Sew down sleeve facings the same way. Carefully steam press garment on WS under a damp pressing cloth. Seam

underarms. Sew on button. Weave in all ends neatly on WS.

Pocket
On right front, pick up and knit 30 sts 1¼ in / 3 cm above the folded edge (= 6 rows from eyelet row). Work 2 rows St st and then work in pattern from Chart 2. Begin pattern on 15th st. Work the sts on each side of pattern in St st.
After completing charted rows, work 2 rows in St st. BO with I-cord as for neck. Sew down pocket along sides with tiny hand stitches.

DRESS FOR SMALL GIRLS

This sweet little dress is sized for newborns to 3-year-olds. The "flame" lace pattern takes a little concentration, but the result is totally worth it.

SKILL LEVEL
Experienced

SIZES
0-3 (6-9, 12-18, 24-36) months

FINISHED MEASUREMENTS
Chest: 17 (18¼, 19¾, 21¼) in / 43 (46, 50, 54) cm
Total Length: 12¾ (15, 17, 19) in / 32 (38, 43, 48) cm

MATERIALS
Yarn:
CYCA #3 (DK, light worsted) Bamboo from Viking of Norway (50% cotton, 50% bamboo rayon, 120 yd/110 m / 50 g)
Yarn Color and Amount:
Natural White 602: 150 (150, 200, 200) g
Needles: U. S. size 4 / 3.5 mm: circular

KNITTING GAUGE
24 sts in pattern = 4 in / 10 cm; 22 sts in stockinette / stocking stitch = 4 in / 10 cm.
Adjust needle size to obtain correct gauge if necessary.
Crochet Hook: U. S. size D-3 / 3 mm
Crochet Techniques: Single crochet (sc)/UK double crochet (dc), slip stitch (sl st), and crab stitch (sc/UK dc worked left to right)

Front and Back
CO 189 (198, 216, 234) sts. Join, being careful not to twist cast-on row; pm for beginning of rnd. Work around in lace pattern following the chart until piece is 8 (9¾, 11¾, 13½) in / 20 (25, 30, 34) cm long. Knit the next rnd, decreasing as evenly spaced around as possible to 94 (100, 108, 118) sts. Work 6 rnds k1, p1 ribbing and then knit 4 rnds. Divide piece for front and back with 47 (50, 54, 59) sts in each piece.

Back
Continue working back and forth in St st. Shape armholes on RS rows by decreasing 1 st at each side a total of 4 times = 39 (42, 46, 51) sts rem. When back is 2½ (2, 2 ¾, 3¼) in / 6 (7, 7, 8) cm past ribbing, bind off the center 15 (18, 18, 23) sts for back neck and work each side separately. BO another 2-2 sts at neck edge (on alternate rows) = 8 (9, 11, 12) sts rem for shoulder. When piece measures 3¼ (3½, 3½, 4) in / 8 (9, 9, 10) cm from ribbing, BO rem sts. Work the other side the same way, reversing shaping to correspond.

Front
Continue working back and forth in St st. Shape armholes on RS rows by decreasing 1 st at each side a total of 4 times = 39 (42, 46, 51) sts rem. When back is 1½ (2, 2, 2½) in / 4 (5, 5, 6) cm past ribbing, bind off the center 5 (8, 8, 13) sts for front neck and work each side separately. BO another 2-2-1-1-1-1 sts at neck edge (on alternate rows) = 8 (9, 11, 12) sts rem

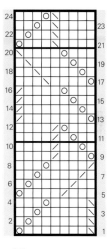

☐   Knit on RS, purl on WS

◹   Sl 1, k1, psso

◿   K2tog

◉   Yo

for shoulder. When piece measures 4 (4¼, 4¼, 4¾) in / 8 (9, 9, 10) cm from ribbing, BO rem sts. Work the other side the same way, reversing shaping to correspond.

Finishing
Join shoulders. Weave in all ends neatly on WS. Turn dress inside out and carefully steam press dress under a damp pressing cloth.

Edging Around Neck and Armholes
Work 1 rnd sc/UK dc around and join with 1 sl st into 1st sc/UK dc. Work a rnd of crab st and join with 1 sl st into 1st sc/UK dc. Cut yarn and fasten off.

SOCKS WITH HARLEQUIN PATTERN

Soft, elegant socks you can wear as bed socks or throw into your bag when heading out for a garden party. They'll be ever so nice and lovely to wear when it gets colder as the evening goes on.

SKILL LEVEL
Experienced

SIZES
Shoe sizes U. S. 5½-6/6½-7 (7½-8/8½-9) / Euro 36/37 (38/39)

MATERIALS
Yarn:
CYCA #1 (fingering) Sisu from Sandnes Garn (80% wool, 20% nylon; 191 yd/175 m/50 g)
Yarn Color and Amount:
White 1001: 100 (100) g
Needles: U. S. size 2.5 / 3 mm: set of 5 dpn

KNITTING GAUGE
27 sts in stockinette / stocking stitch = 4 in /10 cm; 32 sts in pattern = 4 in /10 cm.
Adjust needle size to obtain correct gauge if necessary.
Crochet Hook: U. S. size B-1 or C-2 / 2.5 mm
Crochet Techniques: Chain st (ch), single crochet (sc)/UK double crochet (dc), half-double crochet (hdc)/UK half-treble crochet (htc), double crochet (dc)/UK treble crochet (tr)

With dpn, CO 56 (60) sts. Divide sts evenly onto 4 dpn with 19 sts each on Ndls 1 and 3, and 9 (11) sts each on Ndls 2 and 4. Work in pattern following the chart for Ndls 1 and 3 and work in St st on Ndls 2 and 4. After completing 2½ rep, shape the ankle over Ndls 2 and 4

as follows: K2tog tbl, k5 (7), k2tog. Work 3 rnds and decrease again: K2tog tbl, k3 (5), k2tog. Cut yarn = 48 (52) sts rem.

Heel Shaping
Begin at center back of sock and place 12 (13) sts on each side onto a dpn = 24 (26) sts. Work back and forth in St st for a total of 18 (20) rows, ending with 1 purl row on WS.
Turn heel: Knit until 10 (11) sts rem on needle, k2tog tbl, k1; turn. Purl until 10 (11) sts rem, p2tog, p1; turn. Knit until 9 (10) sts rem, k2tog tbl, k1; turn. Purl until 9 (10) sts rem, p2tog, p1; turn. Continue as est with 2 fewer sts on the needle until all the sts have been worked. End with a WS row.
With RS facing, pick up and knit 12 (14) sts along heel flap, work in pattern across Ndls 2 and 3, pick up and knit 12 (14) sts on opposite side of heel flap. Continuing in the rnd, begin rnds at center of sole.

Gusset
Ndl 1: Knit until 2 sts rem, k2tog.
Ndl 2: Knit and in pattern.
Ndl 3: Pattern and knit.
Ndl 4: K2tog tbl, knit to end of rnd.

Decrease as est on every other rnd until 48 (52) sts rem.

Foot
Work around in St st and pattern until foot measures 7 (7½) in /18 (19) cm.

Toe Shaping
Now work in St st over all sts around.
Ndl 1: Knit until 3 sts rem on needle, k2tog, k1.
Ndl 2: K1, k2tog tbl, knit to end of needle.
Ndl 3: Work as for Ndl 1.
Ndl 4: Work as for Ndl 2.
Decrease as est on every other rnd until 6 (8) sts rem. Cut yarn and draw end through rem sts; tighten.

Crocheted Edging at Top of Leg
Rnd 1: *Ch 3, skip 2 sts, 1 sc/UK dc in next st*; rep * to * around. End with 1 sl st into 1st ch.
Rnd 2: Work (1 sc/UK dc, 1 hdc/UK htr, 1 dc/UK tr, 1 hdc/UK htr, 1 sc/UK dc) in each ch loop around. End with 1 st st into 1st sc/UK dc.
Make the second sock the same way.

Finishing
Weave in all ends neatly on WS. Block socks by laying out (patted out to finished size/shape) between two damp towels. Leave until completely dry.

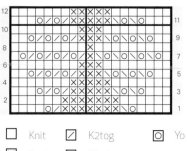

	Knit		K2tog		Yo
	Purl		Sl 1, k1, psso		

PINK BABY BLANKET WITH ANGEL WINGS

This beautiful light blanket with lovely patterns can transformed into a shawl if you make it twice as long. That would mean 16 repeats in length (= 63 in / 160 cm after blocking).

SKILL LEVEL
Intermediate

FINISHED MEASUREMENTS AFTER BLOCKING
27½ x 31½ in / 70 x 80 cm

MATERIALS
Yarn:
CYCA #1 (fingering) Alpakka Silke from Sandnes Garn (70% alpaca, 30% silk, 218 yd/199 m / 50 g)
Yarn Color and Amount:
Pink 3911: 200 g
Needles: U. S. size 2.5 / 3 mm: long circular

GAUGE
32 sts in pattern = 4 in / 10 cm.
Adjust needle size to obtain correct gauge if necessary.

Blanket
CO 207 sts and then knit 1 row on WS. Now work in charted pattern. The repeat is worked 7 times across (+ 10 sts) and 8 times in length. BO. Cut yarn and weave in all ends neatly on WS.

Block blanket to finished measurements (see page 15).

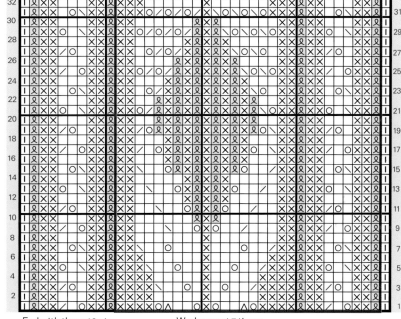

End with these 10 sts   Work repeat 7 times

	▯	Knit on RS, knit on WS
	▢	Knit on RS, purl on WS
	☒	Purl on RS, knit on WS
	℞	K1tbl on RS, p1tbl on WS
	◲	Sl 1, k1, psso
	◱	K2tog
	⊡	Yo
	◮	CDD

GREEN BABY BLANKET WITH LILY LEAF PATTERN

This lovely blanket can also serve as a shawl if you make it twice as long. The beautiful alpaca and silk yarn for this blanket, as well as the pink one on the previous page, elegantly enhances the lace patterns.

SKILL LEVEL
Intermediate

FINISHED MEASUREMENTS AFTER BLOCKING
$28\frac{1}{4} \times 35\frac{1}{2}$ in / 72 x 90 cm

MATERIALS
Yarn:
CYCA #1 (fingering) Alpakka Silke from Sandnes Garn (70% alpaca, 30% silk, 218 yd/199 m / 50 g)
Yarn Color and Amount:
Dusty Green 7741: 200 g
Needles: U. S. size 2.5 / 3 mm: long circular

GAUGE
32 sts in pattern = 4 in / 10 cm.
Adjust needle size to obtain correct gauge if necessary.

Blanket
CO 194 sts and then knit 1 row on WS. Now work in charted pattern. The repeat is worked 12 times across and 9 times in length. BO. Cut yarn and weave in all ends neatly on WS.

Block blanket to finished measurements (see page 15).

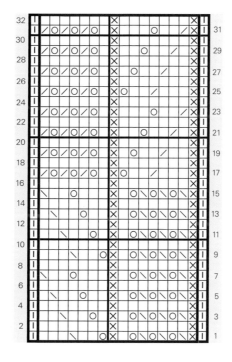

	Knit on RS, knit on WS
	Knit on RS, purl on WS
☒	Purl on RS, knit on WS
⊙	Yo
╲	Sl 1, k1, psso
╱	K2tog

SKIRT WITH LACE EDGING

The lace edging for this skirt is worked back and forth in a long strip and then joined into a ring. Next, pick up and knit stitches along one edge and knit the skirt. We used a cording silk and cotton yarn so the garment would be sturdy and hold its shape.

SKILL LEVEL
Experienced

SIZES
U. S. 8-10 (12-14, 16-18) / Euro 36/38 (40/42, 44/46)

FINISHED MEASUREMENTS
Lower Edge: 39½ (42½, 45¾) in / 100 (108, 116) cm
Hip: approx. 36¼ (39½, 42½) in / 92 (100, 108) cm
Total Length: 19 (20½, 22) in / 48 (52, 56) cm

MATERIALS
Yarn:
CYCA #3 (DK, light worsted) Gamma from Lang Yarns (100% cotton, 180 yd/165 m / 50 g)
Yarn Color and Amount:
Sea-Green 837.0072: 250 (300, 350) g: approx. 32 in / 80 cm long circular
Needles: U. S. size 7 / 4.5 mm
Other Materials: 39½ in / 100 cm waistband elastic, 1¼ in / 3 cm wide

GAUGE
23 sts in stockinette / stocking stitch = 4 in / 10 cm.
Adjust needle size to obtain correct gauge if necessary.

Skirt
CO 18 sts and work in pattern following the chart until the strip is 39½ (42½, 45¾) in / 100 (108, 116) cm long. BO and then seam cast-on and bound-off edges. Pick up and knit 230 (248, 268) sts around one edge. Pm at each side with 115 (124, 134) sts between markers. Work around in St st until skirt measures 7 (8¾, 10¼) in / 18 (22, 26) cm. Decrease at each side as follows: Knit until 2 sts before marker, sl 1, k1, psso; sl m, k2tog. Decrease the same way on every 10th rnd a total of 8 times = 198 (216, 236) sts rem. Continue in St st until skirt is 19 (20½, 22) in / 48 (52, 56) cm long. Purl 1 rnd for foldline. Working back and forth, work 10 rows in St st for the facing.

Finishing
Lay the waistband elastic edge to edge with the foldline on WS, fold down the facing, and sew down with backstitch. Make sure the elastic fits your waist. Machine stitch the ends of the band to join and trim excess.

Turn skirt to wrong side and gently steam press under a damp pressing cloth. Weave in all ends neatly on WS.

☐   Knit on RS, knit on WS

⚕   Twisted knit (k1tbl) on RS, twisted purl (p1tbl) on WS

☒   Purl on RS, knit on WS

☑   K2tog on RS, p2tog on WS

☐   Yo on RS, yo on WS

PILLOW COVER WITH DIAMOND SYRUP COOKIE PATTERN

This pillow cover has lace on the front and stockinette / stocking stitch on the back. It's knitted in one piece and then seamed at the sides and lower edge. Don't forget to leave an opening along the bottom edge so you can insert the pillow form. Finish by hand-seaming the bottom edge.

SKILL LEVEL
Intermediate

FINISHED MEASUREMENTS
15¾ x 15¾ in / 40 x 40 cm

MATERIALS
Yarn:
CYCA #1 (fingering) Stellina from Lang Yarns (55% silk, 45% cotton, 131 yd/120 m / 25 g)
Yarn Color and Amount:
Sea-Green 895.0088: 125 g
Needles: U. S. size 4 / 3.5 mm
Other Materials: pillow form, 15¾ x 15¾ in / 40 x 40 cm

GAUGE
27 sts in stockinette / stocking stitch = 4 in / 10 cm.
Adjust needle size to obtain correct gauge if necessary.

Pillow Cover
CO 108 sts and knit 2 rows.
NOTE: Always knit the first and last st of each row as edge sts.
Continue in St st + edge sts until piece measures 15¾ in / 40 cm.
Knit 1 row on WS as foldline and then continue in charted pattern as follows:
1 edge st, k5, rep charted pattern 6 times, k5, k1 edge st. Work a total of 6 rep in length and then BO.

Finishing
Fold cover at foldline. With RS facing RS, seam the sides with back stitch inside edge sts. Turn cover right side out and insert pillow form. Hand sew the bottom opening closed as invisibly as possible.

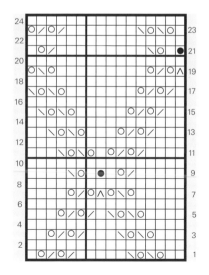

	Knit on RS, purl on WS
⟍	Sl 1, k1, psso
⟋	K2tog
○	Yo
●	Knit 5 into the same stitch alternating knit into front, knit into back of st. Turn and p5. Turn and k5tog.
⋀	CDD

BOOKMARK

If you're an inexperienced lace knitter, here's a little project to let you practice working lace on both right and wrong sides. I like small, useful projects that help me learn something new; that's why I designed this bookmark. If you're as avid a reader as I am, you'll especially enjoy this pretty handmade marker.

SKILL LEVEL
Intermediate

FINISHED MEASUREMENTS
$1\frac{1}{2}$ x 7 in / 4 x 18 cm

MATERIALS
Yarn:
CYCA #1 (fingering) Stellina from Lang Yarns (55% silk, 45% cotton, 131 yd/120 m / 25 g)
Yarn Color and Amount:
Sea-Green 895.0088: 25 g
Needles: U. S. size 2.5 / 3 mm

Other Materials: piece of cardboard or plastic, $1\frac{1}{2}$ x 7 in / 4 x 18 cm

GAUGE
27 sts in stockinette / stocking stitch = 4 in / 10 cm.
Adjust needle size to obtain correct gauge if necessary.

CO 25 sts and work back and forth in charted pattern. Work a total of 10 rep in length. BO. With WS facing WS, sew the long sides together. Insert the stiffener and seam each end.

	Knit on RS, knit on WS
	Knit on RS, purl on WS
☒	Purl on RS, knit on WS
◹	On RS, sl 1, k1, psso. On WS, p2tog tbl
⊙	Yo

LACE TOP WITH SCALLOP MOTIFS

This pretty summer top is knitted with a linen, viscose, and cotton blend which will feel soft and pleasant against your skin. The top is knitted in one piece on a circular needle with raglan shaping up to the shoulders—an interesting way to knit a sleeveless top.

SKILL LEVEL
Experienced

SIZES
XS (S, M, L, XL, XXL)

FINISHED MEASUREMENTS
Chest: approx. 32¼ (35½, 38½, 41¾, 45, 48½) in / 82 (90, 98, 106, 114, 123) cm
Total Length: 20½ (21, 21¼, 21¾, 22, 22½) in / 52 (53, 54, 55, 56, 57) cm

MATERIALS
Yarn:
CYCA #3 (DK, light worsted) Scarlet by Permin (58% linen, 26% viscose, 16% cotton, 164 yd/150 m / 50 g)
Yarn Color and Amount:
White 888003: 200 (200, 250, 250, 300, 350) g
Needles: U. S. sizes 2.5 and 4 / 3 and 3.5 mm: circular and set of 5 dpn

KNITTING GAUGE
22 sts in garter st on smaller needles = 4 in / 10 cm.
22 sts in pattern on larger needles = 4 in / 10 cm.
Adjust needle sizes to obtain correct gauge if necessary.
Crochet Hook: U. S. size D-3 / 3 mm
Crochet Techniques: Single crochet (sc)/UK double crochet (dc) and crab st (sc/UK dc worked from left to right)

Top
With larger circular, CO 180 (198, 216, 234, 252, 270) sts. Join, being careful not to twist cast-on row. Knit 1 rnd. Now work in pattern following chart until piece measures 11 in / 28 cm (all sizes). Change to smaller circular and continue in garter st (= alternately knit 1 rnd, purl 1 rnd). Pm at each side = 90 (99, 108, 117, 126, 135) sts between each marker. After working in garter st for 3¼ in / 8 cm, BO the first 7 (10, 12, 15, 18, 21) sts of the round, work 76 (79, 84, 87, 90, 93) sts, BO 14 (20, 24, 30, 36, 42) sts, work 76 (79, 84, 87, 90, 93) sts, BO 7 (10, 12, 15, 18, 21) sts = 152 (158, 168, 174, 180, 186) sts rem. Cut yarn.

On the next rnd, set up raglan shaping: CO 71 (75, 79, 83, 87, 91) sts for shoulder section (above the bound-off sts), p76 (79, 84, 87, 90, 93) = front, CO 71 (75, 79, 83, 87, 91) sts for second shoulder piece, and p76 (79, 84, 87, 90, 93) = back = a total of 294 (308, 326, 340, 354, 368) sts.
Knit 1 rnd and pm at beginning and end of the sts you cast on for the shoulders = 4 markers. Purl 1 rnd. On the next rnd, decrease 1 st on each side of each marker with k2tog before marker and k2tog tbl after marker = 8 sts decreased per rnd. Rep decreases as est on every other rnd a total of 18

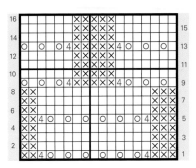

□ Knit
☒ Purl
◎ Yo
4 K4tog

(18, 20, 20, 20, 21) times = 150 (164, 166, 180, 194, 200) sts rem. BO rem sts. Weave in all ends neatly on WS.

Edgings
Ending each rnd with 1 sl st into 1st st of rnd, work 1 rnd of sc/UK dc around neck and then work 1 rnd crab st. Edge each armhole the same way, skipping every 4th st when working sc/UK dc.

SACRED TREE DOUBLE BED COVERLET

When I was little, we rented an old skipper's house in Larkollen, Norway. The bedroom in this photo reminds me of the room in that house where my parents slept. This old coverlet pattern was originally published by Solberg Mill, which kindly granted me permission to include it in this book. Such a lovely pattern certainly deserves to be back in print! It'll take some time to knit the 144 squares on U. S. size 0 / 2 mm needles, but it's worth it—you'll have a bed coverlet to make you happy for many years, and it'll certainly end up a treasured heirloom. The charts can be found on page 138.

SKILL LEVEL
Intermediate

FINISHED MEASUREMENTS
Excluding Edging: approx. 80¼ x 80¼ in / 204 x 204 cm (144 squares, each measuring 6¾ x 6¾ in / 17 x 17 cm)

MATERIALS
Yarn:
CYCA #0 (lace) Solberg 12/4 (100% cotton, approx. 1104.5 yd / 1010 m / 200 g)
Yarn Color and Amount:
White 1002: 2000 g (10 balls)
Needles: U. S. size 0 / 2 mm

GAUGE
Approx. 26 sts in pattern = 4 in / 10 cm. Adjust needle size to obtain correct gauge if necessary.

Square
CO 3 sts and work in pattern following Chart 1, increasing on WS on every other row (see chart). After completing the leaf motif, begin the lace rows following Chart 2, decreasing at each side on every WS row until 3 sts rem. BO.

Make a total of 144 squares.

Chart 2

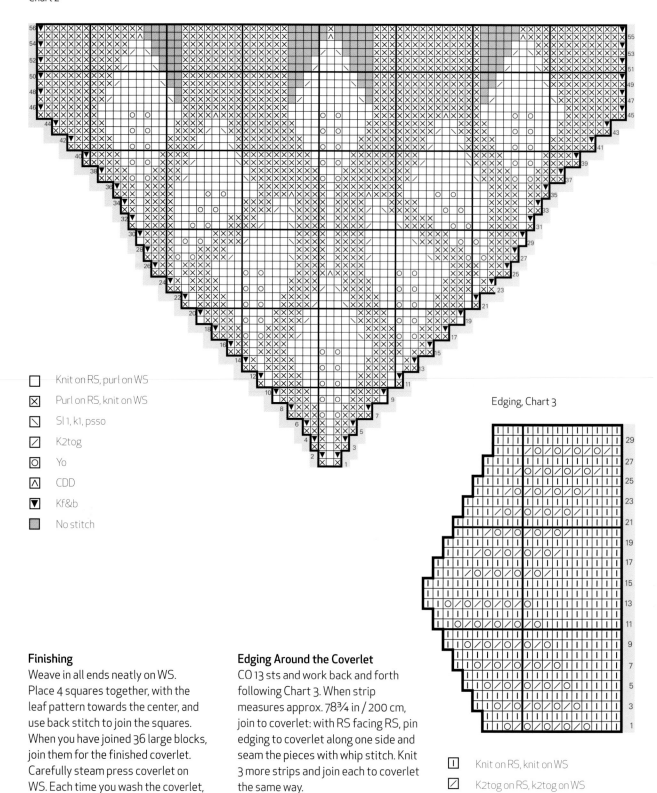

Knit on RS, purl on WS

⊠ Purl on RS, knit on WS

◺ Sl 1, k1, psso

◿ K2tog

◎ Yo

⋀ CDD

▼ Kf&b

▨ No stitch

Edging, Chart 3

Knit on RS, knit on WS

◿ K2tog on RS, k2tog on WS

◎ Yo on RS, yo on WS

Finishing
Weave in all ends neatly on WS. Place 4 squares together, with the leaf pattern towards the center, and use back stitch to join the squares. When you have joined 36 large blocks, join them for the finished coverlet. Carefully steam press coverlet on WS. Each time you wash the coverlet, it will become more beautiful.

Edging Around the Coverlet
CO 13 sts and work back and forth following Chart 3. When strip measures approx. 78¾ in / 200 cm, join to coverlet: with RS facing RS, pin edging to coverlet along one side and seam the pieces with whip stitch. Knit 3 more strips and join each to coverlet the same way.

Chart 2

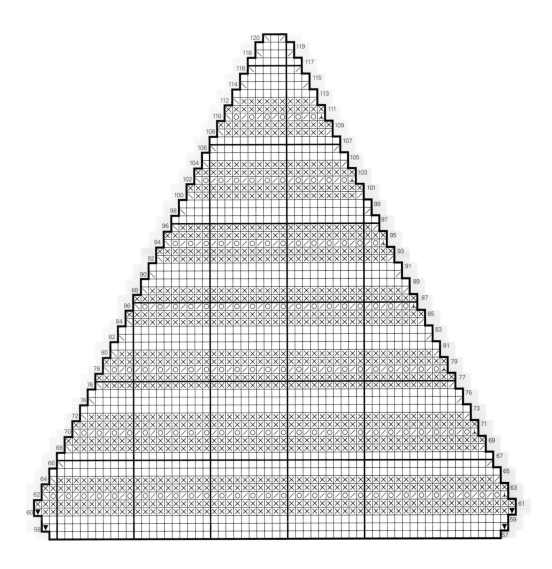

☐ Knit on RS, purl on WS

☒ Purl on RS, knit on WS

▼ Kf&b

◹ Sl 1, k1, psso (worked on WS)

◺ K2tog (on WS)

⊙ Yo (on WS)

⋏ K3tog (on WS)

SOCKS WITH SHELL PATTERN

This pattern is fun to knit, and looks much more complicated than it is! Once you've worked the first few rounds, you'll see that the twisted knit and purl stitches stack over each other neatly—it just doesn't look that way on the chart (page 143).

SKILL LEVEL
Experienced

SIZE
Women's U. S. shoe sizes 7-9 / Euro 37/39

MATERIALS
Yarn:
CYCA #3 (DK, light worsted) Sterk from Du Store Alpakka (40% alpaca, 40% Merino wool, 20% polyamide, 150 yd/137 m / 50 g)
Yarn Color and Amount:
Light Gray Heather 841: 100 g
Needles: U. S. size 4 / 3.5 mm: set of 5 dpn

GAUGE
20 sts in pattern = 4 in / 10 cm.
Adjust needle size to obtain correct gauge if necessary.

Leg
CO 56 sts and divide sts evenly over 4 dpn (14 sts per needle). Join and pm for beginning of rnd. Work in pattern following the chart on page 143 up to the arrow for "shape heel here." Cut yarn. Now work the heel flap back and forth over the sts on Ndls 4 and 1 = 28 sts for flap. Work 14 rows in twisted ribbing: p1, k1tbl on RS and k1, p1tbl on WS (sts are worked knit over knit and purl over purl).

Heel Turn

Row 1 (RS): Work in pattern until 9 sts rem, k2tog tbl; turn.

Row 2 (WS): Work in pattern until 9 sts rem, k2tog; turn.

Row 3 (RS): Work in pattern until 8 sts rem, k2tog tbl; turn.

Row 4 (WS): Work in pattern until 8 sts rem, k2tog; turn.

Continue as est with 1 st less until all sts have been decreased = 12 sts rem.

Gusset and Foot

NOTE: Work in shell pattern over Ndls 2 and 3 but in p1, k1tbl ribbing on Ndls 1 and 4.

Pick up and knit 12 sts along left side of heel flap; work in charted pattern over Ndls 2 and 3. Pick up and knit 12 sts down right side of heel flap. Work in p1, k1tbl ribbing over rem sts. Decrease on every other rnd for gusset:

Ndl 1: Work as est until 2 sts rem, k2tog tbl.

Ndls 2-3: Work in charted pattern.

Ndl 4: K2tog, work in ribbing as est to end of needle.

Decrease the same way on every other rnd until 56 sts rem = 14 sts per needle. Complete charted rows.

Toe Shaping

Now work in p1, k1tbl ribbing over all sts around. Shape toe as follows:

Ndl 1: Work until 2 sts rem, k2tog tbl.

Ndl 2: K2tog, work to end of needle.

Ndl 3: Work until 2 sts rem, k2tog tbl.

Ndl 4: K2tog, work to end of needle.

Decrease the same way on every other rnd until 16 sts rem. Cut yarn and draw end through rem sts; tighten. Weave in all ends neatly on WS. Make the second sock the same way.

← Begin decreasing for toe here

← Shape heel here

ᱺ	K1tbl
⊠	Purl
◲	K2tog tbl
⊙	Yo

LACE BONANZA TUNIC

I've worked a variety of patterns into this pretty turquoise tunic, which can be worn as a long tunic or a short dress. Feel free to lengthen or shorten the garment, but make sure you decrease the correct number of stitches before you begin shaping the armholes. The charts follow on page 147.

SKILL LEVEL
Experienced

SIZES
S (M, L, XL)

FINISHED MEASUREMENTS
Chest: 34¾ (37½, 40¼, 43) in / 88 (95, 102, 109) cm
Total Length: 32 (32¼, 32¾, 33) in / 81 (82, 83, 84) cm
Sleeve Length: 18½ (19, 19¼, 19¾) in / 47 (48, 49, 50) cm

MATERIALS
Yarn:
CYCA #3 (DK, light worsted) Scarlet by Permin (58% linen, 26% viscose, 16% cotton, 164 yd/150 m / 50 g)
Yarn Color and Amount:
Turquoise 888027: 450 (500, 550, 600) g
Needles: U. S. size 4 / 3.5 mm: circular and set of 5 dpn

KNITTING GAUGE
22 sts in stockinette / stocking stitch = 4 in / 10 cm.
Adjust needle size to obtain correct gauge if necessary.

Crochet Hook: U. S. size D-3 / 3 mm

Crochet Techniques: Single crochet (sc)/UK double crochet (dc), chain st

(ch), double crochet (dc)/UK treble crochet (tr), and slip st (sl st)

Body
With circular, CO 323 (340, 357, 374) sts. Join, being careful not to twist cast-on row; pm for beginning of rnd. Work following Chart 1, decreasing evenly spaced around to 288 (304, 320, 336) sts as indicated on chart. Now work following Chart 2, decreasing evenly spaced around to 248 (266, 280, 296) sts as indicated on chart. Pm at each side with 124 (133, 140, 148) sts each for front and back. K6 (3, 7, 4), work 8 (9, 9, 10) pattern rep following Chart 3, k12 (7, 14, 8), work 8 (9, 9, 10) pattern rep following Chart 3, and end with k6 (4, 7, 4). *At the same time,* starting at this point, decrease 1 st on each side of each marker with k2tog before marker and k2tog after marker on every 8th rnd a total of 14 times (until you've completed Chart 5). Be careful not to decrease within the lace pattern. Work in St st at sides as necessary. After completing Chart 3, 228 (246, 260, 276) sts rem. Now set up next pattern: K3 (3, 2, 2), work 12 (13, 14, 15) pattern rep following Chart 4, k6 (6, 4, 3), work 12 (13, 14, 15) rep following Chart 4, and end with k3 (3, 2, 1). As before, do not work decreases into lace pattern. After completing Chart

4, 212 (230, 244, 260) sts rem. Set up next pattern: K3 (2, 6, 5), work 10 (11, 11, 12) rep of Chart 5, k6 (5, 12, 10), work 10 (11, 11, 12) rep of Chart 5, end with k3 (3, 6, 5). Once again, do not decrease at sides in lace pattern. After completing Chart 5, 196 (214, 228, 244) sts rem.
Chart 6 set-up: K1 (1, 1, 1), work 12 (13, 14, 15) rep of charted pattern 6, k2 (4, 2, 2), work 12 (13, 14, 15) rep of Chart 6, end with k1 (1, 1, 1). After completing Chart 6, knit 1 rnd *at the same time* as you decrease 10 sts at each side (= 5 sts on each side of each marker) = 176 (194, 208, 224) sts rem. Set body aside while you knit the sleeves.

Sleeves and Raglan Shaping
With dpn, CO 52 sts (all sizes). Divide sts onto 4 dpn and join; pm for beginning of rnd (= center of underarm). Work 3 pattern rep following Chart 1, ending each rnd with k1. Continue in St st and, *at the same time,* shape sleeve: on every 8th rnd, increase 1 st on each side of marker until there are 72 (76, 80, 82) sts total. Work until length of sleeve to underarm = 18½ (19, 19¼, 19¾) in / 47 (48, 49, 50) cm. BO 10 sts centered at underarm (5 sts on each side of marker) = 62 (66, 70, 72) sts rem. Set sleeve aside and make another the same way.

Place sleeves on circular, matching underarms on sleeve and body = 300 (326, 348, 368) sts. Count out to the center front and BO the center 6 (5, 6, 6) sts. Shape raglan with 1 decrease using 1 st from body and 1 from sleeve at each of the four intersections of body and sleeve = center st of raglan. Begin working back and forth. On RS, *work until 4 sts rem before the first center st. K2tog tbl, work in pattern following Chart 7, once across, k2tog*.

Rep * to * at each of the rem 3 center sts = 8 sts decreased. Decrease the same way on every RS row a total of 26 (28, 30, 32) times = 82 (93, 98, 102) sts rem. BO rem sts but *do not cut yarn*.

Edging
Insert crochet hook into last st of bind-off and work 1 row sc/UK dc on WS around neck and placket. Turn work to RS and work *ch 3, 1 dc/UK tr

in 1st ch, skip 2 sts, 1 sc/UK dc in next st*. Rep * to * across and end with 1 sl st into 1st st. Cut yarn and fasten off ends.

Finishing
Seam underarms. Weave in all ends neatly on WS. Turn tunic inside out and carefully steam press tunic on WS under a damp pressing cloth.

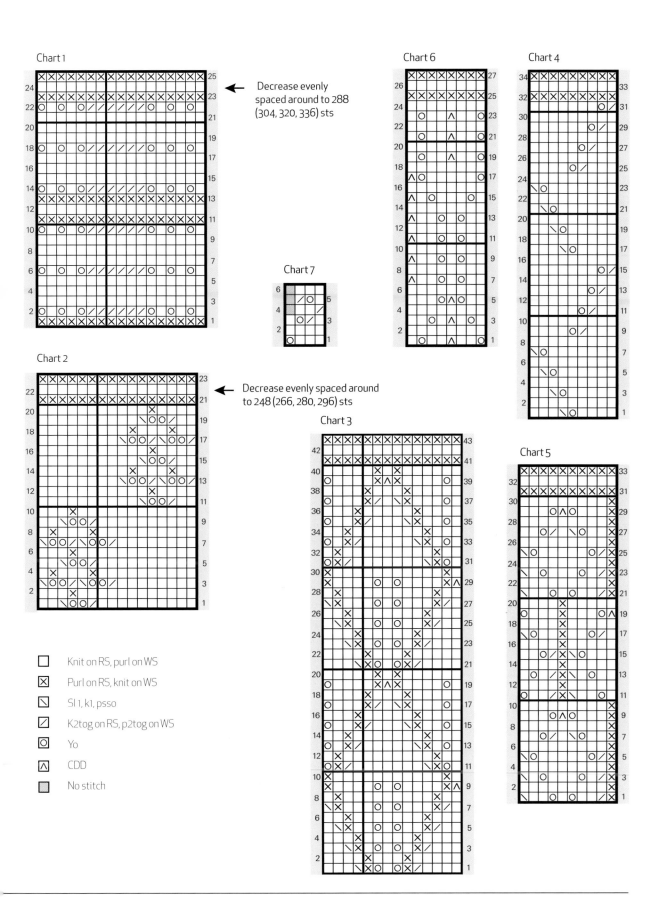

Chart 1

← Decrease evenly spaced around to 288 (304, 320, 336) sts

Chart 7

Chart 6

Chart 4

Chart 2

← Decrease evenly spaced around to 248 (266, 280, 296) sts

Chart 3

Chart 5

- ☐ Knit on RS, purl on WS
- ☒ Purl on RS, knit on WS
- ◲ Sl 1, k1, psso
- ◱ K2tog on RS, p2tog on WS
- ◙ Yo
- ⋀ CDD
- ▧ No stitch

BOLERO WITH GATSBY WAVES

This bolero (named for a vintage 1920s hairstyle) is knitted with a lovely festive sequin yarn, perfect over a party dress or bridal gown. The pattern, decorative in itself, makes natural waves at the bottom edge and front panels. You won't need to add an extra edging or closing at the front. The pattern chart is on page 150.

SKILL LEVEL
Experienced

SIZES
S (M, L, XL)

FINISHED MEASUREMENTS
Chest: $34\frac{3}{4}$ ($37\frac{3}{4}$, $41\frac{3}{4}$, $45\frac{3}{4}$) in / 88 (96, 106, 116) cm
Total Length: $13\frac{3}{4}$ ($14\frac{1}{2}$, $15\frac{1}{2}$, $16\frac{1}{4}$) in / 35 (37, 39, 41) cm
Sleeve Length: $18\frac{1}{2}$ (19, $19\frac{1}{4}$, $19\frac{3}{4}$) in / 47 (48, 49, 50) cm

MATERIALS
Yarn:
CYCA #2 (sport, baby) Novara from CeWeC (40% cotton, 40% microfiber, 20% acrylic, 164 yd/ 150 m / 50 g)
Yarn Color and Amount:
Natural White 01, 300 (350, 350, 400) g
Needles: U. S. size 4 / 3.5 mm: short and long circulars and set of 5 dpn

GAUGE
24 sts in stockinette / stocking stitch = 4 in / 10 cm.
25 sts in pattern = 4 in / 10 cm.
Adjust needle size to obtain correct gauge if necessary.

Body

With circular, CO 219 (241, 265, 291) sts. Working back and forth, knit 2 rows (= 1 garter ridge). Now work in pattern and St st as follows: K1 (edge st), 44 sts charted pattern, 20 (31, 43, 56) sts in St st, p1, 88 sts charted pattern, 20 (31, 43, 56) sts in St st, 44 sts charted pattern, k1 (edge st). Continue as est until piece measures 6¼ (6¾, 7, 7½) in / 16 (17, 18, 19) cm. Divide for front and back: 55 (60, 66, 73) sts for right front, 109 (121, 133, 145) sts for back, and 55 (60, 66, 73) sts for left front. Place each front on a holder and work back.

Back

Shape armhole by binding off at each side 3-2-2-1 sts = 93 (105, 117, 129) sts rem. Work without shaping until piece measures 13 (13¾, 14½, 15½) in / 33 (35, 37, 39) cm. Place the center 39 (41, 43, 45) sts on a holder for back neck and work each side separately. At neck edge, decrease 1-1 sts = 25 (30, 35, 40) sts rem for shoulder. Continue in pattern until piece measures 13¾ (14½, 15½, 16¼) in / 35 (37, 39, 41) cm. Place rem sts on a holder and work the other side to correspond.

Right Front

Shape armhole at right side as for back = 47 (52, 58, 65) sts rem. Continue in pattern until front measures 10¾ (11, 11½, 11¾) in / 27 (28, 29, 30) cm. Place the first 12 (12, 13, 15) sts on a holder for neck. At neck edge, BO 2-2-2-1-1-1-1 sts = 25 (30, 35, 40) sts rem for shoulder. When piece is same total length as back, place shoulder sts on a holder.

Left Front

Work as for right front, reversing shaping to correspond.

Joining Shoulders

Join shoulders as follows: With RS facing RS, slip sts onto needles U. S. size 4 / 3.5 mm. Use a third needle to join shoulders with 3-needle bind-off (see page 107).

Sleeves

With short circular, pick up and knit 91 (95, 105, 115) sts around armhole (skipping about every 3rd st). Pm at center of underarm. Work around in St st and, *at the same time*, every ¾ in / 2 cm, shape sleeve with k2tog tbl before marker and k2tog after marker. Decrease as est until 55 (55, 66, 66) sts rem. When sleeve is 15½ (15, 16 ¼, 16½) in / 39 (40, 41, 42) cm long, work 1 pattern rep following chart. Finish with 2 rnds garter st (= knit 1 rnd, purl 1 rnd).

Finishing

Place sts of left front, back, and right front on circular and knit 4 rows garter st. BO.
Weave in all ends neatly on WS.

Chart legend:

☐	Knit on RS, purl on WS
☒	Purl on RS, knit on WS
⊡	Yo
⧅	Sl 1, k1, psso
⧄	K2tog

CHRISTENING GOWN AND HAT

It isn't easy to calculate precise sizing for a baby to be christened. This christening dress was knitted for a baby about six months old. If the child will be christened earlier, you can adjust the sizing by going down a needle size for both the dress and hat. The charts for the outfit are on page 154.

SKILL LEVEL
Experienced

SIZES
3-6 months

DRESS

FINISHED MEASUREMENTS
Chest: 23¾ in / 60 cm
Circumference at Lower Edge: 51¼ in / 130 cm
Total Length: 37¾ in / 96 cm
Sleeve Length: 6¾ in / 17 cm

MATERIALS
Yarn:
CYCA #1 (fingering) Bambino from Viking of Norway (50% bamboo, 50% cotton, 191 yd /175 m / 50 g)
Yarn Color and Amount:
White 400: 500 g
Needles: U. S. sizes 1.5 and 2.5 / 2.5 and 3 mm: circular and set of 5 dpn (If the child is 3 months old, use U. S. sizes 0 and 1.5 / 2 and 2.5 mm)
Other Materials: 6 buttons + silk ribbon

KNITTING GAUGE
26 sts in pattern and 28 sts in stockinette / stocking stitch on needles U. S. size 2.5 / 3 mm = 4 in / 10 cm.
Adjust needle size to obtain correct gauge if necessary.
Crochet Hook: U. S. size B-1 or C-2 / 2.5 mm

Crochet Techniques: Single crochet (sc)/UK double crochet (dc), chain st ch) and slip st (sl st)
Edge Stitches: On top part of dress, always knit the first and last st of every row.

Front and Back
With U.S. size 2.5 / 3 mm circular, CO 336 sts. Join, being careful not to twist cast-on row; pm for beginning of rnd. Work around in pattern following Chart 1 until piece measures approx. 31½ in / 80 cm. End with a complete rep. To gather the skirt, k2tog around = 168 sts rem. Knit 1 rnd. On the next rnd, work eyelets: (yo, k2tog) around. Work in St st for ¾ in / 2 cm.
Now divide for back and front with 42 sts for each of the back sections and 84 sts for the front. Place each back section on a separate holder and continue on the front.

Front
The top section is worked back and forth in St st. BO 2-1-1-1 at each side for the armhole shaping = 74 sts rem. Continue without further shaping until piece measures 4 in / 10 cm from eyelet rnd. Place the center 28 sts on a holder for neck and work each side separately. At neck edge, on every other row, BO 2-2-1 sts = 18 sts rem for shoulder. When the St st section is 5½ in / 14 cm long, BO rem sts. Work

the other side the same, reversing shaping to correspond.

Left Back
Shape armhole as for front = 37 sts rem. Continue in St st until piece measures 4¾ in / 12 cm from eyelet rnd. Place the outermost 16 sts on a holder for back neck. At neck edge, on every other row, BO 2-1 sts = 18 sts rem for shoulder. When the St st section is 5½ in / 14 cm long, BO rem sts.

Right Back
Work as for left back, reversing shaping to correspond.

Sleeves
With dpn U. S. size 1.5 / 2.5 mm, CO 48 sts. Divide evenly onto dpn and join. Work following Chart 2 a total of 4 times in length. Change to dpn U. S. size 2.5 / 3 mm and St st. Pm at beginning of rnd = center of underarm. When sleeve is 1¼ in / 3 cm long, increase 1 st on each side of the marker. Increase the same way every 1¼ in / 3 cm a total of 10 times = 68 sts. If necessary, space increases more closely together as you near sleeve top. When sleeve is 6 in / 15 cm long, work the rest of the sleeve back and forth, *at the same time* as you BO 2-1-1-1 sts at each side for sleeve cap. BO rem sts. Make the second sleeve the same way.

Finishing and Neckband

Join shoulders. Pick up and knit 104 sts, including those on holders from both back and front. Work in pattern following Chart 2, ending with p2. Work pattern for 4 rep in length. BO as shown on chart with knit over knit and purl over purl. Do not cut yarn, but continue with it to crochet 2 rows of sc/UK dc along one side of the back, skipping every 4th st on 1st row of sc/UK dc to prevent ruffling. Cut yarn and work two rows sc/UK dc along opposite side. Finally, crochet a buttonhole loop: *Ch 3, skip 2 sts and work 1 sl st into 3rd sc/UK dc*; rep * to * for a total of 6 loops. End with 2 sc/UK dc. Cut yarn and fasten off.

Turn dress inside out and carefully steam press garment under a damp pressing cloth.

Sew on 6 buttons opposite button loops. Thread silk ribbon through the eyelet rnd.

HAT

MATERIALS
Yarn:
CYCA #1 (fingering) Bambino from Viking of Norway (50% bamboo, 50% cotton, 191 yd /175 m / 50 g)
Yarn Color and Amount:
White 400: 50 g
Needles: U. S. sizes 1.5 and 2.5 / 2.5 and 3 mm: circular and set of 5 dpn (If the child is 3 months old, use U. S. sizes 0 and 1.5 / 2 and 2.5 mm)
Other Materials: silk ribbon

GAUGE
24 sts in pattern on needles U. S. size 2.5 / 3 mm = 4 in / 10 cm.
Adjust needle size to obtain correct gauge if necessary.

With U. S. size 1.5 / 2.5 mm needles, CO 106 sts. Purl 1 row. Next row, begin pattern: K1 (edge st), rep pattern

Chart 1

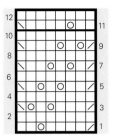

Chart 2

	Knit on RS, purl on WS
☒	Purl on RS, knit on WS
⊙	Yo
⟋	K2tog
⟍	Sl 1, k1, psso

following Chart 2 17 times, end with p2, k1 (edge st). Work a total of 4 pattern rep. Now work following Chart 1: K1 (edge st), rep pattern following Chart 1 13 times, k1 (edge st). When piece measures 4 in / 10 cm (= 3 rep in length of Chart 1), BO the last row on WS as follows: BO 32 sts, work 42 sts, BO 32 sts. Continue in pattern following Chart 1 over the 42 rem sts for back neck, knitting the first and last st of every row as edge sts. When neck section is 4 in / 10 cm long (= 3 rep of Chart 1), BO all sts. Sew the neck section to the bound-off sts at each side.

With U. S. 1.5 / 2.5 mm needles, pick up and knit 94 sts along the edge on RS. Pick up and knit 1 st in every 2 out of 3 sts. Purl 1 row on WS. On next row, work eyelets: K1 (edge st), (k2tog, yo) to last st and end with k1 (edge st). Purl 1 row. Now K1 (edge st), pattern following Chart 2 15 times, p2, k1 (edge st). Work pattern rep a total of 4 times. BO all sts.

Finishing
Cut yarn and weave in all ends neatly on WS. Thread silk ribbon through eyelet row.

RUGGED SWEATER WITH MEDALLIONS

Knit a lace pattern with heavy yarn on large needles for a rugged look. The medallion pattern looks completely different here than on the top of the dress shown on page 106. This sweater knits up quickly in a few evenings. The detached neckband is knitted in the round in stockinette / stocking stitch, so you'll have rolled edges at both top and bottom. The charts are on page 158.

SKILL LEVEL
Experienced

SIZES
XS-S (M, L-XL)

FINISHED MEASUREMENTS
Chest: approx. 40¼ (45, 48) in / 102 (114, 122) cm
Total Length: 22 (22¾, 23¾) in / 56 (58, 60) cm
Sleeve Length: 19 (19¼, 19¾) in / 48 (49, 50) cm

MATERIALS
Yarn:
CYCA #6 (super bulky) Anouk from Lang Yarns (50% alpaca, 50% microfiber, 61 yd/56 m / 100 g)
Yarn Color and Amount:
Mint 776.0072: 800 (900, 1000) g
Needles: U. S. size 15 / 10 mm: short and long circulars and set of 5 dpn

GAUGE
10 sts in pattern = 4 in / 10 cm.
Adjust needle size to obtain correct gauge if necessary.

Body
With circular, CO 102 (114, 122) sts.

Join, being careful not to twist cast-on row; pm for beginning of rnd. Set up pattern: P1 (4, 6), work 49 sts medallion pattern following Chart 1, p2 (8, 12), work 49 sts medallion pattern on Chart 1, p1 (4, 6). Pm at side after 51 (57, 61) sts. Work as est until piece measures 13½ (13¾, 14¼) in / 34 (35, 36) cm. Now divide piece for back and front and work each side separately. Place front sts on a holder.

Back
Continue in pattern as est until piece measures 22 (22¾, 23¾) in / 56 (58, 60) cm. BO.

Front
Work as for back.

Sleeves
With short circular, CO 25 (27, 29) sts; join to work in the round. Set up pattern: P4 (5, 6), work pattern following Chart 2, p4 (5, 6). Pm at center of underarm (= beginning of rnd). When piece measures 2 in / 5 cm, increase 1 st on each side of marker. Increase the same way every 2 in / 5 cm 8 times = 41 (43, 45) sts.
NOTE: Purl all new sts.

Chart 1

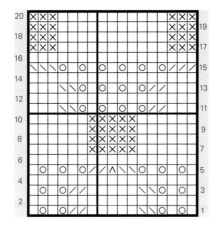

Chart 2

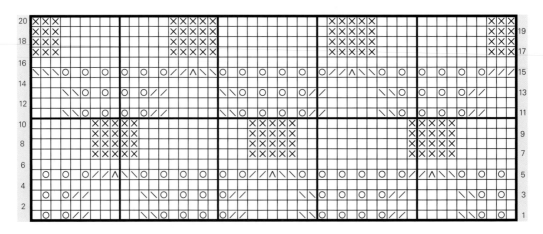

	Knit on RS, purl on WS
☒	Purl on RS, knit on WS
⃝	Yo
⃥	Sl 1, k1, psso
⃫	K2tog
⋀	CDD

When sleeve is 19 (19¼, 19¾) in / 48 (49, 50) cm long (as measured down center of underarm), loosely BO all sts. Make the second sleeve the same way.

Finishing
Join shoulders = approx. 4¾ (5½, 6¼) in / 12 (14, 16) cm for each shoulder = 10¾ (11½, 11½) in / 27 (29, 29) cm neck width.
Attach sleeves.

Detached Neckband
With short circular, CO 50 sts. Join and pm for beginning of rnd. Work around in St st until piece is approx. 7 in / 18 cm long. BO.
Weave in all ends neatly on WS.

LONG LACE SCARF

This scarf is knitted with the Climbing Rose pattern. The kid mohair and silk yarn is so light that the scarf only weighs 1¾ oz / 50 g. It's surprising how much a scarf this weightless will warm your neck.

SKILL LEVEL
Intermediate

FINISHED MEASUREMENTS
Approx. 11 x 71 in / 28 x 180 cm

MATERIALS
Yarn:
CYCA #0 (lace) Kid Seta from Mondial (70% mohair, 30% silk, 230 yd/210 m / 25 g)
Yarn Color and Amount:
Ice-Green 592: 50 g
Needles: U. S. size 6 / 4 mm

GAUGE
20 sts in pattern = 4 in / 10 cm

CO 56 sts and then knit 1 row (1st row = WS). Work in charted pattern until scarf measures 180 cm. BO loosely.

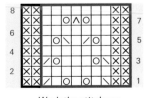

Work the stitch rep
6 times across.

☐ Knit on RS, purl on WS

☒ Purl on RS, knit on WS

◺ Sl 1, k1, psso

◿ K2tog

⊡ Yo

◮ CDD

PONCHO EDGED WITH FAUX CABLES

The body of this poncho is worked in stockinette / stocking stitch, but its fine lace edging gives it a special flair. The edging is worked with doubled yarn to enhance the fine structure of the lace pattern. The poncho is relatively long but you can easily shorten it by reducing the stitch count when you cast on.

SKILL LEVEL
Intermediate

SIZE
One size

FINISHED MEASUREMENTS
Excluding Edging: approx. 25¼ x 32¼ in / 64 x 82 cm for each piece

MATERIALS for Poncho
Yarn:
CYCA #1 (fingering) Mini Sterk from Du Store Alpakka (40% Merino wool, 40% alpaca, 20% polyamide, 182 yd/166 m / 50 g)
Yarn Color and Amount:
Light Gray Heather 841: 400 g
Needles: U. S. size 2.5 / 3 mm: 32 in / 80 cm or longer circular

GAUGE
Approx. 26 sts in stockinette / stocking stitch = 4 in / 10 cm.
Adjust needle size to obtain correct gauge if necessary.

MATERIALS for Edging
Yarn:
CYCA #1 (fingering), Mini Sterk from Du Store Alpakka (40% Merino wool, 40% alpaca, 20% polyamide, 182 yd/166 m / 50 g)
CYCA #0 (lace) Dreamline Soul from Du Store Alpakka (68% alpaca, 32% polyamide, 195 yd/178 m / 25 g)
Yarn Colors and Amounts:
Mini Sterk: Light Gray Heather 841: 150 g
Soul: Light Gray Heather DL203: 50 g

Needles: U. S. size 7 / 4.5 mm

GAUGE
18 sts in pattern = 4 in / 10 cm.
Adjust needle size to obtain correct gauge if necessary.

PONCHO
With circular U. S. size 2.5 / 3 mm, CO 212 sts. Work back and forth in St st until piece measures approx. 25¼ in / 64 cm. BO. Make another piece the same way.

Blocking and Joining
Carefully steam press the poncho on WS under a damp pressing cloth. Sew the short side of one piece along the long side of the second piece. Sew the second short side to the long side of opposite piece so that it forms a V-neck on front and back.

EDGING
With needles U. S. size 7 / 4.5 mm and 1 strand each Mini Sterk and Soul, CO 16 sts. Work in pattern following the chart. **NOTE:** The stitch count varies—it increases to 18 on Row 1 and decreases to 13 sts on Row 9. Work charted pattern until strip measures 57 in / 145 cm; *do not bind off.*
To make sure you've knitted the right length for the edging, pin it, RS facing RS, to the two sides of the lower edge of the poncho. Adjust number of pattern reps as necessary and then BO. Cut yarn. Make another strip the same way. Pin out the edgings as

shown in illustration to right. Dampen well with water and leave until completely dry.

Finishing
With RS facing RS, pin the edgings to the lower edge of poncho and then seam the pieces with 1 strand of Mini Sterk.

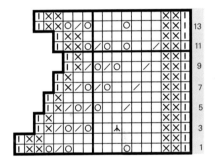

		Knit on RS, knit on WS
□		Knit on RS, purl on WS
⊠		Purl on RS, knit on WS
⊡		Yo
⧄		K2tog
⋏		K3tog

Blocking the edgings

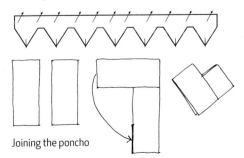

Joining the poncho

PARISIAN PASTRIES GLOVES

My father, who was a master baker, seldom brought home pastries from the bakery. Once, however, he gave us some absolutely wonderful little cakes he called Parisiennes. In France, these cakes are "Prussians." When my gloves were finished, I looked at them and thought of those little cakes. Knitting the fingers isn't as difficult as you might think, but it takes a little time and you have to keep count. When they're finished, you'll have a pair of exceptionally elegant gloves. Knitted in white, they'd be lovely for a winter bride. The pattern chart is on page 166.

SKILL LEVEL
Experienced

SIZES
S/M (L/XL)

MATERIALS
Yarn:
CYCA #1 (light fingering) Dreamline Sky from Du Store Alpakka (70% alpaca, 30% silk, 128 yd/117 m / 25 g)
Yarn Color and Amount:
Light Pink DL306: 50 g
Needles: U. S. size 1.5 / 2.5 mm: set of 5 dpn

KNITTING GAUGE
30 sts in stockinette / stocking stitch = 4 in / 10 cm. Adjust needle size to obtain gauge if necessary.
Crochet Hook: U. S. size 0 / 2 mm
Crochet Techniques: Chain st (ch), single crochet (sc)/UK double crochet (dc), and slip stitch (sl st), double crochet (dc)/UK treble crochet (tr)

Left Glove
With dpn, CO 56 (60) sts. Divide sts over 4 dpn and join. Set up pattern as follows: K2, 29 sts charted pattern (see page 166), St st over next 25 (29) sts. Continue as est until piece measures 4¾ in / 12 cm. On the next rnd, begin shaping thumb gusset. Work increases with yo, which is knitted tbl on following rnd to avoid holes. Increase 1 st on each side of next-to-last st of rnd on every 4th rnd a total of 6 (7) times = 13 (15) sts for thumb. When piece measures 6¾ (7) in / 17 (18) cm, place the 13 (15) thumb sts + 1 st at each side = 15 (17) sts, on a holder. CO 3 new sts over gap = 56 (60) sts. Continue in pattern and St st until glove measures approx. 8 (8¾) in / 20 (22) cm. End with a complete repeat. Knit 1 rnd over all sts around. Place 23 (25) sts for back of hand on a holder, keeping 12 (13) sts on needles for little finger; place rem 23 (24) sts for palm on another holder.

Little Finger
= 12 (13) sts. Divide sts onto 3 dpn and CO 2 new sts between little and ring fingers = 14 (15) sts. Work around in St st for 2¼ (2½) in / 5.5 (6.5) cm. Shape tip: (k2tog) around. Cut yarn and draw tip: (k2tog) around. Cut yarn and draw end through rem sts; tighten and weave in end on WS.

Hand
Place sts from holders onto dpn and pick up and knit 2 sts on inside of little finger = 46 (49) sts. Knit 3 rnds in St st. Divide the 2 sts at little finger + 7 (7) sts on back of hand and 6 (7) sts from palm onto dpn. Place rem sts back on holders = 15 (17) sts for back of hand and 16 (16) sts for palm.

Ring Finger
= 15 (16) sts; CO 1 (2) new sts on side of ring finger = 16 (18) sts total. Work around in St st for approx. 2¾ (3¼) in / 7 (8) cm. Shape tip: (k2tog) around. Cut yarn and draw end through rem sts; tighten and weave in end on WS.

Middle Finger
Move 7 (8) sts from back of hand holder onto dpn + 8 (8) sts from palm holder; pick up and knit 2 sts at ring finger and CO 1 (2) new sts on side of middle finger = 18 (20) sts total. Work around in St st for approx. 3 (3¼) in / 7.5 (8.5) cm. Shape tip: (k2tog) around.

Cut yarn and draw end through rem sts; tighten and weave in end on WS.

Index Finger
Move rem 16 (17) sts from holders onto dpn; pick up and knit 2 (3) sts at middle finger = 18 (20) sts total. Work around in St st for approx. 2½ (3) in / 6.5 (7.5) cm. Shape tip: (k2tog) around. Cut yarn and draw end through rem sts; tighten and weave in end on WS.

Thumb
Divide sts held for thumb onto dpn and pick up and knit 3 sts in cast-on sts on top of gap = 18 (20) sts. Work around in St st for approx. 2¼ (2½) in / 5.5 (6) cm. Shape tip: (k2tog) around. Cut yarn and draw end through rem sts; tighten and weave in end on WS.

Right Glove
Work as for left glove, reversing pattern placement to correspond:

Work in St st over the first 25 (29) sts, work 29 pattern sts, and end with k2. Increase for thumb gusset on each side of the 2nd st of rnd instead of next-to-last st. Make sure to place thumb and fingers correctly for right hand!

Crocheted Edging
Edge the glove cuffs with: 1 sc/UK dc, *ch 3, 1 dc/UK tr in 1st ch, skip 2 sts, 1 sc/UK dc in next st*; rep * to * around, ending with 1 sl st into 1st sc/UK dc.

Finishing
Soak the gloves in lukewarm water and then lay flat until dry. Alternatively, pat out gloves to finished shape/measurements and place a damp towel over the gloves; leave until completely dry.

K1tbl (twisted knit)

Purl

Yo

K2tog tbl

K2tog

CDD

BABY ONESIE

This sweet outfit in the Bee Swarm pattern will suit any baby well. You can extend the ribbing at the lower edges of the legs and sleeves as needed so the baby can wear the garment for more than a week. They grow so fast! The pattern chart follows on page 170.

SKILL LEVEL
Experienced

SIZES
3-6 (6-12, 12-18, 24) months

FINISHED MEASUREMENTS
Chest: 19¾ (22, 23¾, 25¼) in / 50 (56, 60, 64) cm
Leg Length: 8¼ (9, 9¾, 10¾) in / 21 (23, 25, 27) cm
Total Length: 20½ (22½, 24½, 26¾) in / 52 (57, 62, 68) cm
Sleeve Length: 6 (6¾, 7, 8 ¼) in / 15 (17, 19, 21) cm

MATERIALS
Yarn:
CYCA #3 (DK, light worsted) Sterk from Du Store Alpakka (40% alpaca, 40% Merino wool, 20% polyamide, 150 yd/137 m / 50 g)
Yarn Color and Amount:
Light Gray Heather 841: 200 (200, 250, 250) g
Needles: U. S. size 2.5 and 4 / 3 and 3.5 mm: circulars and set of 5 dpn
Other Materials: 6 (6, 6, 7) buttons

GAUGE
22 sts in pattern on larger needles = 4 in / 10 cm.
Adjust needle size to obtain correct gauge if necessary.

Legs
The Onesie begins at lower edge of one leg. With smaller dpn, CO 40 (44, 44, 48) sts. Divide sts onto dpn and join. Work in k2, p2 ribbing for 2½ (2½, 3, 3¼) in / 6 (6, 8, 8) cm. Now knit 1 rnd, *at the same time* increasing evenly spaced around to 65 (69, 73, 77) sts. Pm around the 1st and last sts = marked sts. Always knit the 2 marked sts. Change to larger dpn or short circular and set up pattern: K2 (1, 3, 2), rep 6-st pattern following chart, and end with k3 (2, 4, 3). Continuing in pattern as est, on every 1½ (1½, 1¾, 1¾) in / 3.5 (3.5, 4, 4.5) cm, increase 1 st on each side of marked sts a total of 4 times = 73 (77, 81, 85) sts. Work new sts into pattern when possible. Continue in pattern until leg measures 8¼ (9, 9¾, 10¾) in / 21 (23, 25, 27) cm and then set piece aside. Make second leg the same way. Place sts of both legs onto one circular and pm at center back and center front = 146 (154, 162, 170) sts total. Begin rnd at center back. Continue around following charted pattern, making sure the pattern aligns well. *At the same time*, BO 1 st on each side of marked sts, using k2tog tbl before marker and k2tog after marker, on both front and back. Decrease the same way on every other rnd a total of 8 times = 114 (122, 130, 138) sts rem. BO the center 6 sts at from for opening = 108 (116, 124, 132) sts. From this point on, work back and forth in charted pattern until piece measures 17 (18½, 20, 21¾) in / 43 (47, 51, 55) cm from cast-on edge. Make sure the motifs align and you are knitting the lace rows on RS.
NOTE: Always knit the first and last st of each row as edge sts. The pattern doesn't rep at center back, so work those sts in St st (see photo on page 171).

Shape armholes on WS as follows:
Work 22 (25, 27, 29) sts, BO 6 sts, work 52 (54, 58, 62) sts, BO 6 sts, work 22 (25, 27, 29) sts = 96 (104, 112, 120) sts rem. Set body aside and knit sleeves.

Sleeves
With smaller dpn, CO 32 (36, 36, 40) sts. Divide sts onto dpn and join. Work in k2, p2 ribbing for 2½ (2½, 3, 3 ¼) in / 6 (6, 8, 8) cm. Now knit 1 rnd, and, *at the same time*, increase evenly spaced around to 41 (41, 45, 45) sts. Pm around the 1st and last sts = marked sts. Always knit the 2 marked sts. Change to larger dpn or short circular and work around in charted pattern. *At the same time*, increase 1 st on each side of marked sts every ¾ in / 2 cm a total of 5 (6, 6, 7) times = 51 (53, 57, 59) sts. Work all new sts in St st. Work as est until sleeve is 6 (6¾, 7, 8 ¼) in / 15 (17, 19, 21) cm long, or desired length. You may need to space decrease rnds more closely together near top of sleeve. End on the same rnd as for back and front.

BO 6 sts centered at underarm (= BO 3 sts each at beginning and end of rnd) = 45 (47, 51, 53) sts rem. Make the second sleeve the same way.

Raglan Shaping

Arrange body and sleeve sts on larger circular = 186 (198, 214, 226) sts total. Pm at each of the 4 intersections of body and sleeve. Continue working back and forth in charted pattern and, *at the same time*, on RS rows, shape raglan by decreasing at each marker: work until 2 sts before marker, sl 1, k1, psso, sl m, k2tog = 8 sts decreased around. Decrease the same way on every other row a total of 10 (12, 13, 15) times. Now decrease only on front as possible, and, *at the same time*, BO 3 sts at beginning of every row for the neck until you've decreased for the raglan a total of 14 (16, 17, 19) times. Place rem sts on a holder.

Button and Buttonhole Bands

With smaller circular, pick up and knit 1 st in each st/row along right front for a boy or left front for a girl, skipping every 4th st/row. You'll need a stitch multiple of 4 + 2. Work back and forth in k2, p2 ribbing for 1 in / 2.5 cm, making sure each RS row begins and ends with k2. BO. Work the opposite band the same way, but, when band is 3/8 in / 1 cm wide, make 5 (5, 5, 6) buttonholes. Space buttonholes evenly down band, keeping in mind

that the top hole will be worked into the neckband.

Buttonholes

BO 2 sts and then CO 2 new sts over gap on next row.

Neckband

With smaller circular, pick up and knit 86 (86, 90, 90) sts around neck, including sts on holders. You'll need a stitch multiple of 4 + 2. Work back and forth in k2, p2 ribbing for 1 in / 2.5 cm. Don't forget the last buttonhole, centered on the neckband. BO loosely with knit over knit and purl over purl.

Sew on the buttons. Seam underarms and crotch. Sew down button bands above crotch. Weave in all ends neatly on WS. Fold up the ribbing on sleeve and leg cuffs.

12								11
10							
8	O	V	O					9
O	V	O					7
6 | | | | | | | | 5
4 | | | | O | V | O | | 3
2 | | | | O | V | O | | 1

☐ Knit on RS, purl on WS

O Yo

V Sl 1, k2tog, psso

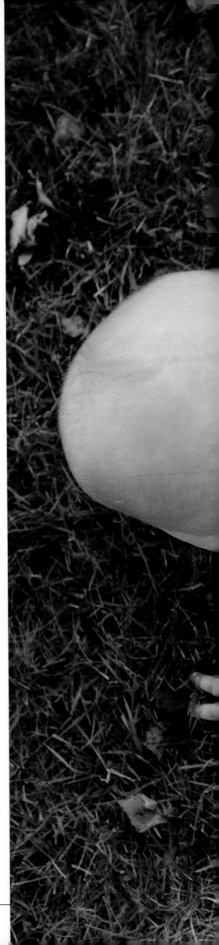

HAT, SCARF, AND MITTENS

Lace on a hat, scarf, and mitten set—really? Won't that be a bit cold? Not at all! There's insulation in the loft of the yarn, and you'll be surprised how comfortable you are. The mittens and scarf are knitted back and forth, while the hat is worked in the round. The scarf stays securely around the neck because one end slides through the ribbed casing on the other end. Charts for the set are shown on page 175.

SKILL LEVEL
Experienced

SIZES
S/M (L/XL)—hat fits head 20½ (22) in / 52 (56) in circumference

MATERIALS
Yarn:
CYCA #4 (worsted, afghan, Aran)
Cotinga from Dale Yarn (70% wool, 30% alpaca, 87 yd/80 m / 50 g)
Yarn Color and Amount
Natural White 0020
Hat: 100 g
Scarf: 100 g
Mittens: 100 g
Needles: U. S. sizes 6 and 8 / 4 and 5 mm: small circular and set of 5 dpn

GAUGE
19 sts in pattern = 4 in / 10 cm.
Adjust needle size to obtain correct gauge if necessary.

HAT
With smaller short circular or dpn, CO 72 (80) sts. Join, being careful not to twist cast-on row; pm for beginning of rnd. Work around in k1 p1 ribbing for 2½ in / 6 cm. Change to larger needles. Work in pattern following Chart 1 until piece measures approx. 6¾ (7½) in / 17 (19) cm. Knit 1 rnd. Continue in St st.

Shape Crown
Change to dpn when sts no longer fit around circular.
Rnd 1: (K6, k2tog) 9 (10) times = 63 (70) sts rem.
Rnd 2: Knit around.
Rnd 3: (K5, k2tog) 9 (10) times = 54 (60) sts rem.
Rnd 4: Knit around.
Rnd 5: (K4, k2tog) 9 (10) times = 45 (50) sts rem.
Rnd 6: Knit around.
Rnd 7: (K3, k2tog) 9 (10) times = 36 (40) sts rem.
Rnd 8: (K2tog) around = 18 (20) sts rem.
Rnd 9: (K2tog) around = 9 (10) sts rem. Cut yarn and draw end through rem sts; tighten. Weave in all ends neatly on WS.

SCARF
With larger needles, CO 9 sts. Work in pattern following Chart 2.
NOTE: Always increase inside the edge sts. Edge sts = at beginning of row: sl 1 purlwise with wyf; at end of row: k1tbl. After completing Chart 2, make a casing. Sl 1, (k2tog, k2) until 4 sts rem, end with k2tog, k1, k1tbl = 25 sts rem.
Work in k1, p1 ribbing inside edge sts for 3¼ in / 8 cm. After completing ribbing, cut yarn and place sts on a holder.

With WS facing, pick up and work 25 sts where previous ribbing began. As before, work k1, p1 ribbing inside edge sts for 3¼ in / 8 cm. Make sure the two ribbed pieces are the same length. Now join the pieces: Work k2tog across joining a st from each needle. The casing is now complete. On the next row, work in pattern following Chart 3 and, *at the same time*, increase evenly across to 33 sts. Continue as est until scarf measures approx. 19¾ in / 50 cm. End with a half repeat. Place sts on a holder.

Make another piece the same way, but after working 3¼ in / 8 cm in ribbing, proceed directly to Chart 3 without picking up sts (since you don't need a casing on this end). Don't forget to increase to 33 sts, as before. Work following Chart 3 until piece measures approx. 19¾ in / 50 cm.

Finishing
Join the two pieces with 3-needle bind-off: Hold the two pieces parallel with RS facing RS. With a third needle, knit the first st of each needle tog. *Knit the next pair of sts together and pass the first st on right needle over the second*. Rep from * to * until all sts have been bound off. Fasten off last st.

Weave in all ends neatly on WS. Lightly steam press scarf under a damp pressing cloth.

MITTENS
The mittens are worked back and forth and then seamed.

Left Mitten
With smaller needles, CO 42 sts and work 10 rows k1, p1 ribbing back and forth. Change to larger needles and work 2 rows St st. Now work in St st and pattern following Chart 4, and, *at the same time*, increase for thumb gusset as follows:

Row 1: K19, increase 1, k2, increase 1, k2, 15 sts pattern following Chart 4, k4 = 44 sts.

Row 2 and all WS rows: Purl.

Row 3: K19, increase 1, k4, increase 1, k2, 15 sts pattern, k4 = 46 sts.

Row 5: K19, increase 1, k6, increase 1, k2, 15 sts pattern, k4 = 48 sts.

Row 7: K19, increase 1, k8, increase 1, k2, 15 sts pattern, k4 = 50 sts.

Row 9: K19, increase 1, k10, increase 1, k2, 15 sts pattern, k4 = 52 sts.

Now there are 10 sts for the thumb. Place these 10 sts on a holder. On the next row, CO 2 new sts over gap = 42 sts. Continue in St st and pattern following Chart 4 as est. After completing charted rows, 36 sts rem.

Shape top of hand:

Row 1: (K2, k2tog) across = 27 sts rem.

Rows 2, 4, and 6: Purl across.

Row 3: (K1, k2tog) across = 18 sts rem.

Row 5: (K2tog) across = 9 sts rem.

Cut yarn and draw end through rem sts; tighten. Weave in all ends neatly on WS.

Thumb
Place the held thumb sts on larger needles and pick up and knit 4 sts from inside of mitten = 2 sts on each side = 14 sts. The first row will be a

little tight to knit. Work back and forth in St st for about 3¼ in / 8 cm from base of thumb.

Shape tip:

Row 1: (K2, k2tog) across, ending with k2 = 11 sts rem.

Rows 2 and 4: Purl across.

Row 3: (K1, k2tog) across, ending with k2tog = 7 sts rem.

Cut yarn and draw end through rem sts; tighten. Weave in all ends neatly on WS.

Right Mitten
With smaller needles, CO 42 sts and work 10 rows k1, p1 ribbing back and forth. Change to larger needles and work 2 rows St st. Now work in St st and pattern following Chart 4, and, *at the same time*, increase for thumb gusset as follows:

Row 1: K4, 15 sts pattern following Chart 4, k2, increase 1, k2, increase 1, k19 = 44 sts.

Row 2 and all WS rows: Purl.

Row 3: K4, 15 sts pattern following Chart 4, k4, increase 1, k2, increase 1, k19 = 46 sts.

Row 5: K4, 15 sts pattern, k2, increase 1, k6, increase 1, k19 = 48 sts.

Row 7: K4, 15 sts pattern, k2, increase 1, k8, increase 1, k19 = 50 sts.

Row 9: K4, 15 sts pattern, k2, increase 1, k10, increase 1, k19 = 52 sts.

Work the rest of the right mitten as for left mitten.

Finishing
With WS facing, use whip stitch to seam the mitten side, stitching into the outermost st on each side. Seam the thumb the same way. Weave in all ends neatly on WS.

Chart 1—Hat

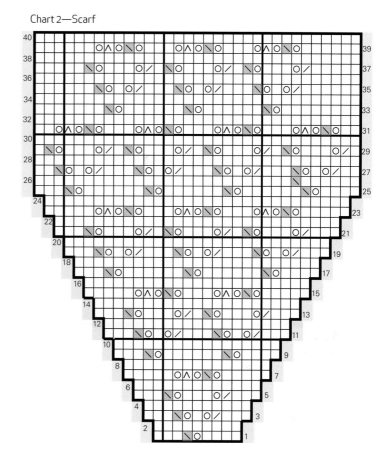

Chart 2—Scarf

Chart 3—Scarf

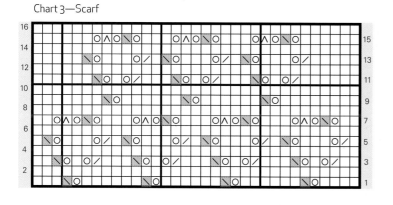

Chart 4—Mittens

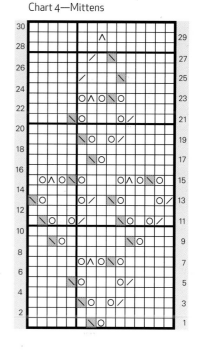

- ☐ Knit on RS, purl on WS
- ⊙ Yo
- ◨ Ssk
- ⧄ K2tog
- ⟑ CDD

YARNS

Cotinga yarn from Dale Garn may be purchased (with international shipping charges) from:
Humble Acres Yarn
www.humbleacresyarn.com

Du Store Alpakka yarns may be purchased (with international shipping charges) from:
Knitting with Attitude
www.knitwithattitude.com

Lang yarns are widely available from yarn stores; see stockists at:
Lang Yarns
www.langyarns.com

Manos del Uruguay yarns are widely available from yarn stores; see stockists at:
Rooster Yarns
www.roosteryarns.com

Permin yarns are selectively available in yarn stores; see stockists at:
Permin
www.permin.dk/uk

Sandnes yarns may be purchased (with international shipping charges) from:
Scandinavian Knitting Design
www.scandinavianknittingdesign.com

Some yarns—CeWeC yarns, Mondial yarns, Solberg yarns, Svarta Fåret yarns, and Viking of Norway yarns, in particular—may be difficult to find. A variety of additional and substitute yarns are available from:
Love Crafts
www.lovecrafts.com

If you are unable to obtain any of the yarn used in this book, it can be replaced with a yarn of a similar weight and composition. Please note, however, the finished projects may vary slightly from those shown, depending on the yarn used. Try www.yarnsub.com for suggestions.

For more information on selecting or substituting yarn, contact your local yarn shop or an online store; they are familiar with all types of yarns and would be happy to help you. Additionally, the online knitting community at Ravelry.com has forums where you can post questions about specific yarns. Yarns come and go so quickly these days and there are so many beautiful yarns available.